Why Women Live Longer Than Men

Why Women Live Longer Than Men

...and What Men Can Learn from Them

Royda Crose, Ph.D.

Jossey-Bass Publishers

The Deserted Rooster and *A Vanishing Species,* by Ric Masten, are reproduced with permission of the author.

Substantial discounts on bulk quantities of Jossey-Bass books are available to corporations, professional associations, and other organizations. For details and discount information, contact the special sales department at Jossey-Bass Inc., Publishers (415) 433–1740; Fax (800) 605–2665.

For sales outside the United States, please contact your local Simon & Schuster International Office.

Jossey-Bass Web address: http://www.josseybass.com

 Manufactured in the United States of America on Lyons Falls Turin Book. This paper is acid-free and 100 percent chlorine-free.

Library of Congress Cataloging-in-Publication Data

Crose, Royda, date.
    Why women live longer than men : —and what men can learn from them / Royda Crose. — 1st ed.
       p.   cm. — (The Jossey-Bass psychology series)
    Includes bibliographical references and index.
    ISBN 0-7879-0340-X
      1. Longevity—Sex differences.   2. Aging—Sex differences.
    3. Health behavior.   4. Women—Health and hygiene.   I. Title.
    II. Series.
    RA776.75.C76   1997
    612.6'8—dc21   96-50433

FIRST EDITION
HB Printing   10 9 8 7 6 5 4 3 2 1

~~~ Contents

Preface   ix

1 **Growing Old in a Changing World**   1
Conventional Wisdom About Longevity • Nature Versus Nurture • Change in Life Expectancy • Living Alone • Why Live Long? • Changing Women in Changing Times • Unchanging Men in Changing Times • A New Vision for Gender Equality in Old Age

2 **Biology, Development, and Longevity**   22
Sex and Gender • Biological Influences on Longevity • Developmental Influences on Longevity • An Integrative Perspective on Longevity

3 **Health and Wellness: Taking Care of Ourselves**   36
Approaches Toward Health • A Model for Wellness • Gender Differences in Wellness

4 **Physical Health: Our Bodies, Our Lives**   55
Reproductive Health • Gender Differences in Health Habits • Physical Health and Longevity

5 **Mental Health: Our Minds, Ourselves**   75
Emotional Expression • Intellectual Development • Differences in Late-Life Learning • Mental Health and Longevity

6 **Social Health: Our Relationships, Ourselves**   94
Competition and Cooperation • Power and Sensitivity • Marriage • Friendship • Caregiving • Support Systems • Relationships and Longevity

7 **Occupational Health: Our Roles, Ourselves**   111
*Role Identity • Traditional Occupational Roles
• Breaking the Bonds of Traditional Roles • The
Economics of Occupational Health • Economic
Resources, Role Continuity, and Longevity*

8 **Spiritual and Environmental Health: Ourselves in
Context**   126
*The Spiritual Dimension • Gender and Religion
• The Environmental Dimension • Leaving Legacies
• Spirituality, Environment, and Longevity*

9 **Living Long and Loving It**   140
*Challenges • Power, Privilege, and Impotence
• Characteristics of Long-Lived People • Role Models
for Living Long and Well • Choices*

References   159

Further Resources   165

About the Author   169

Index   171

—⁓— **Preface**

Freud notwithstanding, I have never wanted to be male. Perhaps this has been a result of growing up in an extended family of females. Perhaps anyone with relatively good self-esteem feels this way about his or her role in life. In any event, at all stages of my life, I have been happy and relieved to be a female. Though I have encountered disadvantages and discrimination at times, I have loved being a woman.

As I age, I keep wondering if that will change. I hear that men get more distinguished and women just get old, but I wonder if that is really the case. Now, after studying and working in the fields of gerontology and psychology for many years, I've come to believe that I'll be as glad to be a woman in late life as I have been at earlier ages. Although women generally have more limited economic resources than men and often suffer from chronic health conditions, many old women report that they have enjoyed greater freedom, life satisfaction, and mental health as they age. In addition, we know that women live longer than men. Why? That is a question that has intrigued me for several years.

The older I become, the more my life seems to be surrounded by women. Most of my women friends are single and looking for new ways to build relationships. Many are building new careers or are only midway in developing a career path. They are learning how to invest money and they worry about building retirement resources. They cannot imagine returning to the type of relationships they once had, where they depended on a husband and paid little attention to the world outside their homes. My women friends are excited about learning, growing, and becoming more involved with a variety of life experiences.

Few men my age are single—and those who are seem to look for younger women to recapture the relationships of their past. Women who have ever looked at the personal ads in the newspapers become discouraged because most men (no matter what their age or physical condition) are advertising for women who are young, slender, and devoted to the interests of the man. This excludes a large portion of the female population, especially those who are over forty.

Some men I know remarry and have a second set of children, with whom they are more connected than they were with the first set. Men my age talk about retirement and disengagement from their work lives. Many want less involvement with work and responsibility and more leisure. They may have ample financial resources for retirement but they seem less excited about their midlife options than my women friends.

This gender gap at midlife and beyond is resulting in multitudes of single women who have resigned themselves to living alone, but who are forming new communities for living together without men. Look around and observe the groups of women who meet for lunch, take trips, or work on projects together. How many groups of older men do you see gathering in restaurants for casual lunches, taking extended vacations together, or simply meeting for potluck dinners or bridge parties? It appears that although men seem to want more leisure and less work, they are not as successful as women are at organizing a variety of activities with friends in old age.

I became interested in issues of aging around the time that I became a grandmother. I was only forty-one years old at the time and not ready to be relegated to the older generation. I got a job working with a Retired Senior Volunteer Program (RSVP) in New York City and began learning about the creativity of older retirees. One of the issues in working with these volunteers was the difficulty in recruiting men. I was awarded a special grant to find ways to interest men in volunteer work. This was my introduction to sex differences among retired people. During this time, I also became interested in promoting mental health for older adults and decided to go back to school to get a doctorate in psychology. It was in my doctoral studies that my life as a feminist took root and I began to study gender differences in development.

Later, as a practicing psychologist specializing in geriatric health care, I noticed that most of the residents of nursing homes are women. I also noticed that most of the participants in community programs for retired people are women. Not only were women living longer and needing more health care, but they were staying active and more involved than men in old age. In my research and my clinical practice, I realized that women are better able to live alone and to take care of themselves in old age. Women experience less loneliness and have more friends. I began to ask the questions "Why do women age differently from men?" and, ultimately, "Why do women live longer?"

To me, these questions seemed very relevant to understanding late-life experiences. But few others seemed to notice. The gerontologists usually focused on the aging population as a whole, without making sex or gender differentiation, while the feminists seemed to believe that women's issues cease to exist after menopause. Gerontologists brushed off my questions as irrelevant. Feminists treated them as boring. It has only been recently that these two groups have begun to take notice of gender differences in aging and to treat these questions seriously.

My natural curiosity and professional drive for inquiry have caused me to search for answers to gender differences in aging. Along the way, I have discovered that women develop critical skills and strengths during the life course that men do not, and I wonder if some of these factors may be contributing to women's greater longevity. Older women seem to be more engaged with the simple things in life. During a workshop on family dynamics, a sophisticated, well-known retired scholar and leader complained, "My wife and daughter are able to talk for hours about nothing. I don't know how they find so much to talk about!" He went on to describe how lonely and disengaged he had become since he had been "pushed out" of his work at a major university at age seventy. Now he was lonely in his retirement because he could not tolerate a conversation with another person if the encounter was not something he perceived as important and worthwhile.

Most women are more connected with friends and family than their male contemporaries. I often ask college students whom they talk to when they call home. "I talk to my mother except when I need money" is invariably the answer I get. Women wear many hats from dishwasher to breadwinner to caregiver to volunteer and can usually name several close friends as their confidantes. These multiple roles and relationships are blessings in late life when roles and friends are often lost. A man tends to focus on one primary role at a time and to rely exclusively on his spouse for intimacy. When he loses either his job or his spouse, he has no backup. He must search desperately for replacement roles and relationships.

Women's lives have been changing over the past decades in ways that bring greater self-esteem, health, and well-being. Men's lives have not been changing in the same way. For many years, we have been raising consciousness about the damage done to women in a patriarchal society where men hold the power, but few have stopped to question the damage that such a society may be doing to men as well.

As women have struggled for more control over their lives and more options for alternative roles, we have redefined femininity. As women have changed, men have become increasingly confused about their own roles and masculine identities. While women have begun to juggle work, home, family, and community responsibilities, men's lives continue to focus primarily on work and retirement. While women are usually caregivers, first for children and then for older spouses and aging parents after their children are grown, most men continue to leave it up to women to do the bed and body work for dependent or sick members of the family. Thus women tend to build networks of friends and family for support, and men tend to depend on their wives to take care of their basic needs for companionship, health care, and emotional support. Most men have few reciprocal relationships outside the workplace, so they lose most of their friendships when they retire.

In their confusion about what their roles should be, some men cling tenaciously to macho images of invulnerability, power, violence, and dominance. The demands of sustaining these images lead some men to self-destructive behaviors—Type A hostility and aggression, alcohol and drug abuse, cigarette smoking, and denial of pain or illness. Men feel required to engage in impulsive, violent behaviors to avoid being considered wimps. These damaging behaviors start very early in life and continue throughout the life span. There is less stigma for a girl to be called *tomboy* or *daddy's girl* than for a boy to be labeled *sissy* or *momma's boy*.

In this youth-oriented society, dominance, invulnerability, and power over others are threatened as one grows old. For men whose lives have been created around old images of masculinity, old age brings despair and disempowerment. Interestingly, the white, able-bodied, heterosexual men who hold the most power, respect, and dominance in this country are the very people who have the highest suicide rates in the country once they pass sixty-five years of age.

Thus the sex roles that we learn in childhood appear to set up patterns that either serve us well or diminish us in old age. Undoubtedly, our genetic heritage plays a significant role in determining how long we will live, but in modern times most people die of illnesses caused by destructive lifestyles—and it is in these things that women seem to be doing better than men.

Some men are intent on resisting the change in women and actively seek methods to legislate and control society so as to return to the "good old days" when women had to live by men's rules. This results in resentment and rigidity, two attitudes that are detrimental to aging well. Thankfully, we have begun to see men who are seeking new ways to be masculine and reclaim their differences from women in more positive ways. A few are asking important questions about how they can learn to break out of the limitations of old sex roles and patterns, to build better relationships and support systems, and ultimately, to live as long as women.

For several years, I have worked with colleagues Neil Schmottlach, David Gobble, and Donald Nicholas to develop a multidimensional systems model for wellness over the life span. In our work, we attempt to study health in the wider context of all life dimensions. We believe that quality-of-life issues depend on more than just physical health. Quality of care and quality of life should always include the emotional, social, intellectual, occupational, spiritual, and environmental aspects of health and well-being as well as the physical. The framework of such a model for wellness helps me better understand the various aspects of gender differences in aging and gives me a method of conveying my insights to others. The concepts that I present here are based on the various life dimensions as I have come to think of them and to use them in my teaching and my life.

There are many ways to think about holistic health. The model for this book emphasizes that life is multidimensional and that everyone has unique ways of living that bring optimism, excitement, and well-being—or disillusionment, illness, and despair. Gerontologists now believe that although personality stabilizes after we reach adulthood, continued adaptability and creativity are the ingredients for living a long, successful, and productive old age.

My goal has been to write a book that will serve to validate women's experiences and struggles for equality and at the same time caution men to consider some of the ways in which they might benefit by changing to be more like women. My perspective is that of a psychologist. Human development and multidimensional health and wellness are what I know best, thus these are the windows through which I look to find answers to my questions.

I am painfully aware that my perspectives as a white woman may not always fit women of color, just as my perspectives as a female and as a clinician will be offered in a voice different from that of males or other empirical scientists. Although I have traveled to several other countries and questioned people from different cultures, my ideas have been primarily formed in the culture of the United States and therefore may not hold true for other settings and contexts. I only hope that my views have some truth for you and help you find ways to increase your own well-being throughout your life span.

Throughout the book, I use quotes and life histories of people I have known, interviewed, or counseled to illustrate the different aspects of longevity and well-being. Names and other identifying factors have been changed to protect the confidentiality of these individuals, except in those cases where I have received specific permission to use true identities. By describing these real-life examples, I hope to show you that it isn't pills, diets, exercises, or good genes that ensure longevity but rather it is the complex combinations of biology, health behaviors, and the many learned and conditioned human characteristics that set the stage for a long life. And many of these life-enhancing learned and conditioned human characteristics are currently more prevalent among women than among men.

ACKNOWLEDGMENTS

I knew I wanted to write a book, but I didn't know how to go about it. Then I happened to sit down next to a man with a sandwich at a session of the 1994 convention of the American Psychological Association. During that chance encounter, Alan Rinzler, senior editor for Jossey-Bass Publishers, not only gave me half his sandwich but also offered to work with me on my book idea. My sincere thanks to Katie Levine and Alan Rinzler at Jossey-Bass, who have known when to encourage, prod, or lie low throughout the process of writing. I feel fortunate to have found them.

My role models, mentors, and subjects for research are the elders I have known, counseled, and studied. They inspire, teach, and relate to me in ways that give special meaning to my life's work. Some of them are the people in this book. My colleagues, David Gobble, Donald Nicholas, and Neil Schmottlach, are the originators of the multi-dimensional systems model for wellness that I use. My work is an expansion and application of their ideas.

The book would never have been completed in a timely fashion if it were not for an excellent support staff at Ball State University. Elan Cohen has been my enthusiastic research assistant, spending much time in the library, looking up articles, sorting out my notes, and helping with my research. He and Letha Collins conducted some of the interviews with elders that are described here. Idona Compliment, Judy Kasey Houlette, Renée Zucchero, and Carrie Speck kept the Center for Gerontology running smoothly so that I had time to devote to writing.

My friends and family have been my support system, cheerleading squad, and gentle critics. I am extremely grateful to Carole Campana and Joan Banks, who read all my early drafts and gave me constructive feedback. They questioned my metaphors and assumptions while they corrected my punctuation and syntax. Reggie Cox and Shirley Pearson gave me a cozy hideaway in Santa Fe where I could write without disturbance.

My daughter, Cynthia Brix, is my best friend and most enthusiastic supporter. She keeps me alive and well in more ways than I can list. My grandchildren, Patrick and Emily Fischer, keep me grounded and balanced by providing love, joy, and family fun on a daily basis. My mother, Pearl Crose, my son, Scott Brix, my daughter-in-law, Kim, and my grandchildren, Ryan and Holly, send me love and support from a distance. I am blessed with much love from many sources and that gives me courage to pursue my goals and follow my dreams.

February 1997   ROYDA CROSE, PH.D.
                                                   Muncie, Indiana

To
My mother, Pearl
My children, Cynthia, Scott, and Kim
My grandchildren, Ryan, Holly, Patrick, and Emily,
And all the men who have significantly influenced my
life, including
Roy, Loyd, Oscar, Don, Nick,
Hank, David, Michael,
Robert, John,
Nicky, and Jack

Why Women Live Longer Than Men

CHAPTER ONE

Growing Old in a Changing World

ake heed, men. In the game of life, women are winning by about seven years. Women are living between 5 percent and 10 percent longer lives, so by very old age there are close to three women for every man. By age eighty-five, most men have expired; many women are living well into their nineties and are increasingly becoming centenarians.

It is curious that scientists rarely note or study the gender gap in aging and that men do not demand to know why they can't live as long as women. Surely men would like to live longer and certainly most women would like to keep men around, so why has so little been done to understand this phenomenon? What are women doing differently and what are the lessons in longevity that men might learn? If stockbrokers were offering 5 percent to 10 percent more interest on investments, people would line up to learn their secrets and emulate their strategies, so it's baffling that men are not knocking down the doors, demanding to learn the secrets of longevity from women.

CONVENTIONAL WISDOM
ABOUT LONGEVITY

For several years, I have been posing the question "Why do women live longer than men?" I've asked students in my classes and friends and colleagues over dinner or during professional meetings. I've asked people I meet on the street, on trains, on airplanes. I've asked audiences at conferences and older adults in senior centers.

The answers typically fall into two distinct categories. Answer number one goes something like "It's hormonal; it's biological" or "It must be in the genes." Answer number two is simply "Men work harder than women" or "Women have less stress than men." Answer number one often comes from the better educated, more politically correct people, who probably know better than to give answer number two as an explanation—even if they believe it to be true. Answer number two is typically given by men but sometimes by older women. Almost everyone seems intrigued by my question and will often give me opinions, but few have given it much thought beyond these rather simplistic answers.

During a singles group where I asked the question, one man, around forty years old, summed it up in a more thoughtful way: "It's obvious—women are smarter than men because they will ask for help. If a woman has to move a big, heavy box, she will wait until someone comes along who can help her. But if a man has to move a big, heavy box, he'll kill himself trying to move it alone and will refuse help even if it is offered."

NATURE VERSUS NURTURE

The biology-hormonal-genetic answer is appealing because it relieves us of responsibility or control of our fate. We can leave our destiny to God or medical science and continue to live our lives without examination or consideration for change. The biological folks can hope that a "fountain of youth" remedy or pill will be developed to extend life, once the mystery of genetics and hormones has been uncovered. The people who feel this way may also believe that nature can be helped along by attending to physical fitness through exercise, nutrition, and healthy lifestyles. On the whole, however, they think that women have the biological advantage and therefore there is little that men can do to live as long as women.

The hard-work-and-stress believers place more value in external, cultural, and behavioral determinants. This view satisfies the work ethic and validates the patriarchal, sexist stereotypes that women have life easy and reap the benefits of men's labor. Men must go out into the world to fight the battles and protect the women and children, while women get to stay at home, safe and unstressed, living in comfort and leisure.

The people holding this view have the idea that things will change as women begin to work like men. Then women will suffer the consequences of stress and hard work that men have endured for so long. When that happens, women will begin to die earlier. They'll realize that their move toward equality has a price to pay. The people who explain gender differences in longevity with the hard-work-and-stress answer rarely entertain the notion that men might live longer if they would begin to be more like women. They assume that because women are striving for equality, they will begin to be more like men and the longevity gap will close in a negative way, resulting in shorter life for women.

Which view is right? Both answers have some truth but both are short-sighted and pessimistic. In reality, we don't yet have exact, scientific proof to explain why women live longer than men. We have the demographics but can only understand the lives of men and women in the context of differing experiences and dynamic characteristics. So what are the differences in men's and women's lives? Let's begin by looking at how our experiences have been changing over the past fifty years.

CHANGE IN LIFE EXPECTANCY

Our gender difference in longevity has emerged only in the past five decades. In the early part of this century, life expectancies for men and women were essentially the same. At birth both sexes could expect to live, on average, to be around forty-nine years old. Now life expectancy has been extended to around seventy-five years, an increase of more than twenty-five years. Medical science and technologies have succeeded in keeping us alive in spite of childhood diseases, complications of pregnancy and childbirth, infections, and accidents, conditions from which young people used to die. We are now living into old age because we survive the traumas of youth.

At the turn of the century, life expectancy for men at birth in the United States was 47.9 years and for women it was 50.9. Fifty years later, in 1950, the averages had extended to 65.6 years for men and 71.1 years for women. The 1990 census reports show the figures are 72.0 years for men and 78.8 years for women.

We arrive in this world in approximately equal numbers of males and females, but we leave it at disproportionate rates. In 1990, there were 1,572,511 girls and 1,644,801 boys less than one year of age in this country. Males continue to have the slight advantage in numbers until around age twenty-five, when the females catch up and begin to outnumber the males. By ages sixty to sixty-four, there were 5,669,120 women and 4,947,047 men—and among those eighty-five years and older, there were 2,222,467 women and only 857,698 men.

With the growing numbers of older adults, it is estimated that there will be one person over the age of sixty-five for every child below the age of twenty-one in this country by the year 2030. And even though there will be both boys and girls born in approximate equal numbers, the widening gender gap will ensure that the adult population, especially the expanding aged population, will be primarily women. This will undoubtedly have major influences on our society.

Many older people today remember when it was common for their siblings and their parents and grandparents to die at early ages.

"Few families had all their children survive then," says Dan—age ninety-two—who remembers when life expectancy was less than fifty years. "I met a woman the other day who said that she had thirteen children. I asked her how many were still living and she said only one had died. I told her she was blessed." Dan's father died at age forty-five from "a busted gall bladder." "That wouldn't happen today," Dan says sadly.

I have been privileged to meet many people in their eighties, nineties, and hundreds who are relatively healthy and active. It is not uncommon to find such active elders living together in residential retirement communities. In these communities, the seventy- and eighty-year-olds are considered to be the youngsters and they will typically point out the centenarians in their group.

"There's a woman in our exercise class that is 102. She can kick her feet just as high as the rest of us. Of course, we are all sitting in a chair when we do it," laughs Bertha, an eighty-two-year-old resident of a retirement village.

While it used to be the exception for anyone to live beyond eighty years old, we now have 3.5 million people aged eighty-five and older—and will add another million by the end of the century. In fact, people more than eighty-five years of age are the most rapidly growing segment of our population.

More than thirty thousand people in the United States are one hundred years old and over. There are so many people now living to be centenarians, it's been estimated that if Willard Scott of the *Today Show* acknowledged all the people celebrating their hundredth birthdays, he would need at least one whole show each week to simply read off their names.

Another indicator of the numbers of people living to be a hundred is found on the racks of greeting card stores, where you can now find printed cards designating eightieth, eighty-fifth, ninetieth, ninety-fifth, and even hundredth birthdays. Evidently the greeting card industry is ahead of the general public in recognizing that there are numbers great enough to constitute a commercial market targeted to people in these advanced ages.

LIVING ALONE

The lifestyles of men and women become increasingly different with age because of the preponderance of women who are widowed and live alone. Every year, the American Association for Retired People publishes a brochure titled *A Profile of Older Americans.* It consistently reports that women are living longer and more independently than men in our society.

The gender gap in widowhood is even greater than the gender gap in longevity for several reasons. Women tend to marry older men who die first. The men who do outlive their wives usually get married again to younger women, and older women who would like to remarry cannot find eligible men. Thus many women spend the last years of their lives as widows. In fact, among people over sixty-five, more than 75 percent of the men and less than 45 percent of the women are married. Close to half of women older than sixty-five live alone. Most of the other half live with spouses or other relatives. Very few live in institutions or with nonrelatives.

There are fewer widowers than widows. When men survive or divorce a spouse, they often marry again very soon. The men who reach advanced ages typically live with a spouse or with other relatives. Few live alone and even fewer live in institutionalized settings.

Men have higher incomes and better economic resources than women, but this is expected to change as women enter the workforce and earn pensions and retirement benefits in their own right, rather than relying on the benefits of their husbands.

Contrast seventy-five-year-old Abe's marital situation with that of Abigail, a widow who is several years older and who lives alone.

Abe retired at age sixty-two and thought he and his wife would have many years to travel and to do all the things that they enjoyed together. Then she got cancer and died. He was lost without her. He could not take care of the big house they had shared together and felt it was too lonely to live there by himself, so he moved to an apartment close to the campus of the local university. He chose this location because he could go to the library to read the newspapers and use the university exercise facilities to keep in shape.

It was not long before he met Donna, a neighbor who was a university professor. She was thirteen years younger and had never been married. They began chatting when they ran into each other in the hallway and soon learned that they had some common interests. Although he was apprehensive at first, he asked her to have dinner with him and that was the beginning of a romance.

While he was still grieving for his wife, he found new vitality with Donna. His relationship with her brought him into the university network and got him involved with new people and new activities. At first, she was not really interested in marriage and liked keeping her own apartment, but she loved the companionship that Abe provided and the attention he gave her, so after an extended courtship she agreed to marry.

Now, at seventy-five, Abe has been married for eight years. He and his second wife are living in a house they designed and built together. When Donna retires in a few years, Abe hopes that he will finally get to travel to all the places he had planned to see with his first wife.

Eighty-four-year-old Abigail has lived alone in her large home since her husband died more than fifteen years ago. They had lived in many places as his work required frequent relocation. They selected this house on a small acreage for their retirement. Now it seems much too big for her alone, but she enjoys entertaining friends for potluck dinners and Sunday afternoon teas. Her children all live in other parts of the country, so this large house is important to her because it provides plenty of room for her many children and grandchildren to come for extended visits. Although she never worked outside her home, she has a comfortable income from her husband's pension. She has remodeled the basement into a small apartment, which she rents to a college student in exchange for help around the house and yard.

Abe and Abigail are both enjoying life in their advanced years, but their living arrangements, lifestyles, companionship, and daily activities are very different. Such remarriage patterns of older men and devotion of older women to family and friends are typical of many of the older people I know.

WHY LIVE LONG?

Ageist attitudes in this youth-oriented society distort the images of aging to be very negative and hopeless. Such images lead younger people to believe that it would be better to be dead than old. In my experience, however, few people among the oldest old want to be dead. From talking to, counseling with, and observing people in advanced ages, I have learned that the experience of old age is typically not what we think it will be when we're younger.

"If I could be younger again," says hundred-year-old Mary, "I think I'd like to be seventy." Amazed at this revelation, my class of graduate students asks, "Why seventy?" "Because I would get to see my great-grandchildren grow up and I'm curious about how they're going to turn out!"

"Well, I wish I could be about ninety again," says ninety-six-year-old Peter. "Then I would still be able to do all the things I've had to give up in the past few years."

My students had expected that such aged people would long to be much younger. They were startled to learn that these elders do not desire to be young again; they like their lives and only wish that they could live longer so they don't miss out on anything.

I can remember when I was twenty-five years old; I thought then that it would be horrible to be fifty, that my life would be essentially over by that point. Now that I am well over fifty, I realize that we never know what any age is like until we reach it. True, being old is different from being young, but for many it's much better than they had imagined and for some it's even better than their youth. Our associations of age with disease, disability, and death prevent us from recognizing and studying the vitality and richness many people enjoy in late life. Women, in particular, often feel that they find new freedom and power in old age.

Years ago, when I was directing a volunteer program for retired people, I met a remarkable woman who opened my eyes to this phenomenon.

After her husband died, Betty began to do volunteer work. All her life had been devoted to her family. She had reared five children, worked alongside her husband in their neighborhood grocery store, and been a traditional housewife. Once she began volunteering, she discovered potential that she had never known before. She learned new skills. She met new people. She won the "volunteer of the year" award. Her community work and even her picture were featured in the local newspaper. Betty was a star for the first time in her life at the age of eighty-one.

Men, too, may find that life in old age—without the pressures to perform and be responsible for others—affords many pleasures that they were denied in their youth. I am often inspired by people like Brian.

Brian enjoyed the freedom to spend his days writing about his varied interests and his keen observations. All his life he had been responsible for others, as a husband, a father, and a minister. His work required him to read and express his ideas from the pulpit, but now, in retirement, he could write about what he wanted rather than what he must. He wrote letters to people around the world and counted many authors and other famous people among his friends, not because he had met them in person, but because he had admired their work and begun to correspond with them. He wrote short stories about the processes of aging and the people he knew. Even after suffering a stroke that left him paralyzed, he continued to type out letters with one finger. On my last visit with him, before his death at age eighty-eight, we edited a speech he had made at a conference on aging, in preparation for its publication.

Brian loved the attention that he received in old age. He would chuckle when he reported that his daughter had once told him, "You weren't very interesting until you reached eighty-five." In response to younger people who would ask him, "Are you keeping busy?" he would always reply, "No! Must I?"

For those who have relatively good health and adequate resources, late life is proving to be truly golden. Many of the oldest people in our society, however, are not as fortunate as the ones I have described so far. There are many who live with chronic illness and less-than-adequate resources, yet most of them—particularly the women—find satisfaction and contentment in late life in spite of such difficulties. I marvel at elders who find ways to live in awareness, love, and self-fulfillment and continue to enjoy life to the very last moment, no matter what their circumstance. They accept the reality of adversity and death, but they continue to embrace life to the very end.

CHANGING WOMEN IN CHANGING TIMES

The oldest-old are people who have lived through very different life experiences from those of the younger women and men of today. Women, especially, have lifestyles, health care, and societal pressures very different from the ones their mothers and grandmothers experienced. Men's lives have changed somewhat but not so dramatically as women's and the results are beginning to show with the increasing gender gap in longevity.

The changes in women's lives appear to be working well. As women's roles have changed, more women are in the workforce and are gaining economic benefits for retirement that our foremothers never had. With more options for life roles, many women now enjoy greater flexibility by being able to work in a lifelong career, stay at home with the children, return to school, work part time, or work intermittently throughout life. Now that medical technology has reduced the risks of death from childbirth, women are living long enough to address other health problems such as osteoporosis, rheumatoid arthritis, and dementia. New treatments for these problems in old age are being developed and there is hope that these chronic illnesses will be conquered as well. With the promise that hormone replacement is offering for women past menopause, there is every indication that—with these improvements in economic re-sources and health care—the gap between women and men will widen in the years to come unless men take heed and begin to make changes in their lifestyles.

The Very Old

Our traditional stereotypes are based on the aging of people now in their eighties and nineties who grew up in the societal upheaval of two world wars, the economic deprivation of the Great Depression, and limited methods of transportation, communication, and medical intervention. Many lived in rural America and few had college edu-cations. They married young, had many children, and never expected to live so long. Few (especially women) had pensions, retirement programs, medical insurance, or savings to last throughout such long lives. Their investments were in their homes and their children. There-fore, staying in their homes or living with their children continue to be of highest value to them.

When today's oldest-old women were turning fifty, their histories and their lives were very different from the current wave of fifty-year-old women. Women who are now eighty and ninety grew up with mothers who never had the right to vote, who had never been employed outside their homes, and who had devoted their lives to their husbands and families. In those days, the mother's major con-tributions to life were considered to be over once the family was grown. These daughters were born at a time when the Civil War was still fresh in the minds of their grandparents, World War I was the war of their fathers and boyfriends, and World War II would be the war of their husbands and sons. The men went to war and the women took care of things on the home front. For these oldest-old women, this may have meant managing farms and small family businesses with which they had been familiar before the men left for service. When I visit a nursing home and ask these women about their past, they often say, "We were farmers!" They rarely say, "I was a housewife." They remember themselves as partners with their husbands and take pride in the work they did. Those who were housewives found volunteer work as a source of satisfaction.

Ninety-one-year-old Rose remembers her work with the Red Cross during the Second World War. Her husband was a business executive and too old to serve in the war, so he stayed in his job and she began to do volunteer work. Before the war began, she had been a socialite with a housekeeper and gardener. She had no children and little to do. The Red Cross became her vocation. As she looks back on her life, this experience was a high point and leaves her feeling that she made a significant contribution.

The Newly Old

The younger groups of elder women, ages sixty-five to eighty, were the brides of the Second World War, the women who entered the factories of an industrialized nation when their husbands, fathers, and brothers left to serve the country. These were not jobs that were familiar or that had even been open to them before the national crisis of war. These were responsibilities that were new to them, and as a result, this generation of women gained a vision beyond the limited roles of wife and mother. They learned new skills, met new friends, and made money in their own right. Mildred and Gladys are examples of women from very different backgrounds whose lives were affected in significant ways during that period of history.

Mildred was a middle-class, educated housewife whose marriage was stable and who longed to be useful, especially as she was childless and not able to fulfill her expected role as mother.

Mildred sold war bonds as her contribution toward the war effort. She worked as a postmistress and proudly reports that she sold more than $250,000 in war bonds to her customers. After the war was over, she returned to her former role as wife and homemaker. She never had children, but she and her husband "adopted" a child through the Big Brothers program. They took him on vacations with them and became a significant influence in this young boy's life. She has been widowed now for many years and lives alone. The young boy she helped stops by to see her on occasion but because she has no children she relies on a younger sister and her friends for a support system.

At times she looks back on her life and wishes that she had continued to work in her job as postmistress, "but it just didn't seem right at the time." The men came back to reclaim their jobs and a postmistress was not appropriate when the postmaster had returned.

Although she worked a number of years, she does not have a pension in her own right now that she is eighty-nine years old. "We made the mistake of cashing in my retirement money because we needed it for other things," she regrets. "Although it did not seem like much at the time, it could have been a good sum of money after all these years and could help me out now that I'm a widow and living on a small income from my husband's Social Security money."

———◆◆◆———

Gladys came from the working class, lacked much formal education, and had a rather unstable marriage.

"Fifty to seventy women retired from the factory at the same time in 1975 after the union got the law, 'thirty years and out,'" says Gladys, an ex–factory inspector. She was referring to a new policy negotiated by the union that allowed workers with thirty years seniority to retire with a pension. Born in 1921, she dropped out of high school and married at age fifteen. Her husband was twelve years older and was a factory worker. After the Pearl Harbor attack and men were going to war, his company got a deferment for him because he was skilled at operating a machine vital for the production of bullets and other war materials. Gladys hired on at several factories before finally getting a job where her husband worked. She stayed there for thirty-one years until she retired at age fifty-two.

"I had some rough jobs . . . really rough . . . awful heavy work . . . I didn't last long on those," she remembers. "I could run most all the machines the men did. One day my machine sent sparks out and set my socks on fire." She chuckles as she recalls her days on the assembly line. Her thought processes seem slow, and it is difficult for her to recall some of the aspects of her life then. She suffers from Parkinson's disease and has pain from arthritis in her knees. "I never thought of leaving the job, though I did think about leaving my husband because he would not work steady and would go off on hunting trips and drink a lot with his buddies," she says. "I was just glad at those times that I had money of my own. When he would take off, I would go out and buy something that I wanted. That's how I got my stereo and my bedroom set. If I wasn't working, I couldn't do that.

"There were times when I wished I could stay home, especially when my youngest daughter was in high school and having some trouble, but most of the time I liked to work. The union had a women's auxiliary, kind of like a club. We would meet once a month and have women-only holiday parties. I still keep in touch with some of the women and we visit when we can.

"After I retired, I got my GED and planned to go to nursing school, but I found out that if I made too much money I would lose some of my pension benefits, so I just got a job at the hospital as a nurse aide and was careful to not go over the amount that I could make and still get my benefits." Gladys feels happy that she has been able to put one granddaughter through nursing school, the job that she had dreamed of for herself.

When the soldiers returned from World War II, there was a lot of pressure to entice or force women to return to hearth and home and to stay out of the workplace. Women's magazines and television commercials stressed the importance of women's work in the home. The housewife dressed in high heels and starched apron, with a sparkling house, kids, and clothes, was promoted as the ideal woman. "Ring around the collar" was the sign of disgrace for the women in detergent commercials. A raft of books supported this effort to get women back home and out of the workplace.

An example of such a book is *The Natural Superiority of Women* by Ashley Montague. In spite of its title, this book, published in 1950, was deceptively subversive to women. While professing to support women and chastise men for their insensitivity and poor treatment of women, Montague glorified the "natural" role of women as mothers and denounced women who didn't wish to follow their "superior" destiny as nurturers to the children and men of the society.

Such pressures resulted in the production of a record number of children, now referred to as the *baby boom*. Women fulfilled their role of becoming mothers as they had in earlier times, only now the babies and the women survived the trauma of childbirth and lived to change society in dramatic ways during the coming decades. These mothers of the baby boom generation, the wives and daughters during the Second World War, are the women who suffered "the problem that has no name" that Betty Friedan wrote about in *The Feminine Mystique*. "The problem lay buried, unspoken, for many years in the minds of American women. It was a strange stirring, a sense of dissatisfaction, a yearning that women suffered in the middle of the twentieth century in the United States. Each suburban wife struggled with it alone. As she made the beds, shopped for groceries, matched slipcover material, ate peanut butter sandwiches with her children, chauffeured Cub Scouts and Brownies, lay beside her husband at night—she was afraid to ask even of herself the silent question—'Is this all?'" (p. 15).

These dissatisfied women were at the forefront of the women's movement toward equality in this country. These women, who will be living many years longer than the men of their generation, are the coming generation of the oldest-old.

Though many women returned to being housewives after the war, some continued to work outside the home, full time, intermittently, or on a part-time basis. They had grown up in a world where women had the vote, and now they were learning that they could make contributions that went beyond their ability to parent and keep house. An unrest at the limitations imposed on women emerged when men returned from the war and expected women to resume their former places in society.

Many of those women who "followed their destiny"—as Montague and others promoted—sought consolation by getting involved in volunteer work but then found themselves alone with no marketable skills at midlife.

> Sixty-three-year-old Suzanne married shortly after graduating from high school. She and her husband had six children and represented the ideal family with a mom at home and a dad providing a good lifestyle. Until Suzanne was fifty years old, she had the American dream, or so she thought. She took care of the home and her husband brought home the money. She was a liberal thinker and a social activist in the volunteer work that she did. Then her husband announced that he wanted a divorce to be free to marry a younger woman. With one child still at home, Suzanne found that she was left to fend for herself. With no college education and no work experience, she was panicked about how she was going to cope.
>
> After some hard times, she now, at age sixty-three, feels good about her life and her independence. She has a secure job that provides health care and a retirement plan, though it pays very little. She belongs to several women's groups that provide companionship for such things as travel, fitness, and investments. She owns her own home and is planning for retirement. "I worry whether I will have enough money to last the rest of my life, because I got a late start," she says. She has no benefits coming to her for all the time she devoted herself exclusively to her home, her family, and her volunteer work.

The Emerging Old

The women who are now in the fifty to sixty-five age range include the dynamic women who led the women's movement as it gained momentum. Most have been employed at some time in their lives. They have more education than previous generations of women and they have explored options beyond that of wife and mother. Many have been divorced. Some have never married. Some are "out" lesbians. Most are obsessed with staying young. They have returned to school in record numbers and continue to pursue higher education as nontraditional students after their families have grown or after they have been divorced or widowed.

For example, in the graduate program in Applied Gerontology that I administer, the majority of students are women and the average age is forty-five, meaning that many of our students are women well over fifty. The oldest student I have had was eighty. Most of these women are already working in the helping professions and return to school to advance their careers or to move in a new direction.

These women have not had the expectation that they needed to do it all at younger ages, so they are coming into their own at midlife after their families have grown. They are discovering themselves as independent and creative older women apart from their family caregiving roles. These are the women of my generation and I know their stories very well—they are similar to my own. We are experiencing satisfaction from our achievements and our friendships with other women but at the same time we are struggling with health issues and wondering about our intimate relationships and prospects for the future.

The life stories that follow are composites of my own friends and acquaintances, who exemplify some of the struggles of midlife women with midlife health, occupational, and relationship dilemmas. For example, Meg has been angry and discouraged but has found peace and direction after surviving a life-threatening disease.

Meg taught school when her kids were little, but she wanted to be a lawyer. When they got old enough to be on their own, she went to law school. She now works in the legal department of a large corporation.

At age fifty-one, she has survived a battle with breast cancer, has recently divorced, and is hoping for grandkids, which neither of her children seems ready to provide. Her job pays well but she feels she is not part of the "good old boys' system" that surrounds her in her chosen profession. She admits she is lonely, but doesn't know quite what to do with her life now that she has achieved success. "I don't know what the next chapter of my life will bring, but I do know I have found myself in this process and I feel good about that," she says. She has maintained friendships with old college classmates and is organizing a support group for women like herself to explore the possibility of building a retirement commune for women.

———✎✎✎———

In her middle years, Amy is facing health and financial problems. After three marriages, in which she was always caregiver to her husbands, she has finally found a loving relationship with a woman who provides support and care during this time of her life.

Amy, at fifty, had put off a needed hysterectomy for several years because she couldn't afford health insurance. Finally, when she started hemorrhaging, she could delay no longer and was rushed to the hospital for emergency surgery. The medical bill for the hospital, the doctors, and the surgery totaled over $12,000, which she didn't have. She had to make arrangements for extended payments and for special waivers for help with these bills. Although her third husband left her with some money after his death, much of that money has been exhausted with living expenses and in helping others in her family who are also having financial and health problems.

In the past few years, Amy has been the primary caregiver for her husband, mother, father, and a brother as they were all terminally ill, and also for a son who is struggling with a life-threatening cancer. Her own health and her jobs have been damaged by these responsibilities.

Amy works as a waitress with no benefits or health insurance. Though she desperately needs to work to pay her bills, she also needs time off to recover from her surgery. Luckily, Carolyn, her life partner, can fill in for her on her job until she gets back on her feet. Amy is glad to have finally found a loving, caring relationship with a partner who is also willing and able to take care of her when she needs help. In most of her other relationships, Amy has always been the caregiver. It is nice to finally have someone who can reciprocate.

Many of these midlife women represent what is coming to be called "the sandwich generation"—people who continue to assume responsibility for teenage, college-age, or young adult children while at the same time working and caring for long-lived relatives of the older generation. They're truly the generation of women who have bridged the change from the old femininity to the new feminism. They're no longer content to be only the nurturing grandmothers waiting at home for their children to visit, but they do stay connected to family in a variety of ways and are responsible family caregivers. They remember and honor the lives of their grandmothers and mothers but are determined that their old age will be different from that of the generations before.

As a result, this generation is learning to take charge of its own health care and to make demands for more research on women's health and high-quality treatment for themselves and their older parents. These women are looking for ways to add life to their years as medical science continues to add years to their lives.

The Aging Baby Boomers

As the first wave of baby boomers turn fifty, old age is beginning to look much, much different from their stereotypes. Many of these boomers are experienced at living in groups, in urban settings, often in apartments, condominiums, or college dormitories. They have much more education, have married later, and have produced fewer children than their parents. They may never have owned a home—or may have owned many, as they moved from place to place in a mobile society. They have enjoyed fringe benefits such as health care and pension plans. They expect to live long and relatively disease free through medical intervention. They believe in finding that elusive "fountain of youth" through diet, pills, surgery, and sheer determination a la physical fitness regimens.

At thirty-five, Chelsea is a woman at the tail end of the baby boom. She is trying to do it all. She is finishing her degree in journalism, volunteering at her children's school, running three or more miles every day, and staying politically active on women's issues. She married at age nineteen and has moved with her husband to three different states and five different homes. Since her divorce two years ago, she transports her two kids three hours to their father's home every other weekend.

At times, she feels angry that she helped her ex-husband through a graduate degree, then when it was her turn to go to college, he deserted her. At other times she feels as if she is just now coming into her own and is discovering life for the first time. She loves the knowledge she is gaining from her classes and the vitality she feels when she meets an interesting new man. She is in better physical shape than ever. For the first time, she has hopes and dreams for herself. Before, they were all for her husband's career.

She has built a strong support system of friends, many of whom are single parents like herself. Luckily, her ex-husband is paying child support and her mother helps out with the kids—and sometimes with money when things are tight. Chelsea's future looks bright, if she can just survive the stress over the next few years until she finishes her degree and the kids are grown.

Such baby boomer women were too young to participate in the early struggles of women's fight for recognition and equality. They and their mothers have had the vote and have been employed in work outside the home. They expect and demand more as equals in a society that continues to discriminate against women. They are entering the political arena and upper management circles and are taking the lead in breaking through the "glass ceiling."

In young adulthood, baby boomer women demanded better and safer contraception to control their pregnancies. They wanted and obtained the right to abortion. Now they are demanding discourse, research, and treatment for menopause as they enter middle age. These women are very different from their grandmothers and their great-grandmothers, who are now living in the nursing homes of this society. By the time they begin needing nursing home care themselves, they will be demanding services and treatment that are not presently available. The long-term care industry will have to change to be ready for this wave of baby boomer women.

UNCHANGING MEN IN CHANGING TIMES

These past fifty years have produced many changes in women's lives, in aging, and in longevity. But what has been happening for men? Very little, when compared to the changes in the lives of women. Although there has been no men's movement to compare with the women's movement, men's jobs have changed with the industrialization of society, and men are benefiting from an increased life span and better medical care. However, few people are seriously questioning men's roles, beliefs about masculinity, and the addictive and aggressive behaviors that damage men and shorten their lives as well as those of women.

Men have been much slower than women to recognize the benefits of changing old patterns and roles. Though some individual men are becoming more involved with the work of the home and the family, there is little evidence of any major societal change in men's roles.

Women continue to do the bulk of the housework, child care, and elder care.

An old-style masculinity is still alive and well and most men have not questioned the harm it does to their own well-being. The macho male image, as portrayed by Clint Eastwood and Sylvester Stallone, is more popular than ever, promoting lifestyles and attitudes that don't lend themselves to care, nurturance, or longevity. Violence, disconnection, and risk-taking delusions of invulnerability are not the ingredients for long life, yet these are the role models that little boys grow up with and that adult men measure themselves by.

"Fighting is fun," says eleven-year-old Randy. He is responding to his grandmother's question about why he gets in so many fights with other boys.

"Yes, but you get hurt and end up crying at home," she responds. "What could be fun about that?"

He replies, "Well, you see, if I don't fight the kids will make fun of me so I make myself get real mad, then it doesn't hurt as much."

Boys like Randy are suffering and their health is at risk. Their models of masculinity are too often drawn from images in the media and from peer pressure, rather than from positive learning experiences of strong, nurturing masculine influences within loving relationships.

Traditional masculine identities are also at risk in today's work environment. Men are retiring from lifelong careers earlier than ever before and have many years of life left in which to grow and develop in new ways. Most men, however, are ill prepared for the isolation and the feelings of worthlessness that retirement can bring. Men's work is usually the root of their power, their productivity, and their self-esteem. The workplace may be the source of their closest friendships. Many men are surprised when they lose much more than the stress of their jobs after retirement. They may find that they have given up the core of their being. The effects of such losses are seen with men's increasing rates of depression with age.

Mark was caught in an identity crisis after retirement. He decided that life was not worth living if he could not be the involved, vital, respected, man-in-control that he had been during earlier times in his life.

Mark had been a successful businessman until his heart condition worsened. He decided to retire and turn over the company to his son. He looked forward to traveling and spending time in a summer home on the coast with his wife. Between trips, he didn't know what to do with himself so he would go down to the business to "help out." His son didn't mind at first, but after a while his father's memory problems began to present problems with customers. Finally, his son asked him not to "help out" anymore. Soon, Mark's memory and confusion became worse. His wife and doctor agreed that he should not be driving. The loss of his work and then the loss of his car were devastating. His wife complained of his dark, gloomy moods, in which he became verbally abusive to her and difficult to live with.

On his last trip, Mark fell in the plane. He was bitterly embarrassed at the resulting scene. Then his doctor told him that his heart condition was inoperable and that his memory condition would not improve. After talking with his wife and his children, Mark decided to quit taking all medication. He lasted just two weeks without the medicine that was keeping him alive.

Of course, women also experience depression with health problems and life changes, but women seem to have more depression in earlier stages of life; their depression, as well as suicide attempts, decrease with age.

As women make more changes in their lives to gain better health, economic resources, and more options for life roles, I predict that the gender gap in longevity will widen even further unless men begin to make equally dramatic changes in their lives. The pessimistic predictions that women will adopt the maladaptive, life-threatening behaviors of men don't seem to be coming true. So it's my sincere hope that the gender gap will narrow because men will change to catch up with women, rather than vice versa.

Medicine and biology can only account for and control a portion of our health and longevity. Our personal attitudes, lifestyles, and connections are what keep us alive in the face of misfortunes beyond the reach of science. Women are demonstrating ways to overcome the limits they have faced in the past. It's in the best interest of men to do the same.

A NEW VISION FOR GENDER EQUALITY IN OLD AGE

How can women, the supposedly weaker and more dependent sex, be winning in the game of life, and men, the stronger and more dominant sex, be dying off at earlier ages? There must be something going on that does not satisfy the typical biology-genetics or work-stress answers that most people have been relying on to explain gender differences in longevity.

There are some important indicators about differences in growth and development, in patterns of relating, in lifestyles, and in attitudes that may help men find answers to life extension. In the past fifty years, women have broken out of the traditional roles of an old femininity that limited their lives. During this same period, a longevity gap between women and men has grown so that women are living significantly longer than men. While there is no conclusive empirical evidence that these two events are related, it is a phenomenon that is interesting to consider.

My own conclusion is that it's time for men to break out of the life-threatening bonds that traditional masculinity places on their lives and their longevity. While I love women and enjoy their friendship, wisdom, and companionship, and think that a world full of old women might be wonderful, I also love men and am deeply concerned about my male friends, my son, and the future of my grandsons if new ways of being masculine are not found so that men too can live long and healthy lives.

In addition to good genes and good health practices, there are many other key ingredients for long life. From the few examples of long-lived people I have given in this chapter, you can see that these individuals are connected with others, engaged with life, flexible in sex roles, and resilient in coping with adversity.

I am convinced that women are living longer than men because women are, by and large, more engaged, connected, flexible, and resilient. In this book, I focus on these ingredients as I develop a theory of life-span wellness that is complex, dynamic, and promising not only for life extension but for life enrichment. It is my intention to promote health and well-being in all aspects of life so that both women and men may live not only longer but better lives.

CHAPTER TWO

Biology, Development, and Longevity

~~~

We come into this world with natural endowments inherited from our biological parents. We find ourselves in an environment that either nurtures us toward a healthy life or blocks us from achieving good health. Our biological programming and our culture interact to cause us to live long or to die early. Men and women have essentially the same environments, the same body parts, the same genetic codes, but we are dying at different rates.

Statistics tell us that those people who have female chromosomes and anatomy are living longer than those with male chromosomes and anatomy. However, these sex differences in mortality rates do not tell us about the other characteristics of the people who live longest. Since some women die early and some men live longer than most women, there must be some traits or behaviors that long-lived people have in common regardless of sex. Is it female sexual biology or is it feminine gender characteristics that enable women to live longer than men?

SEX AND GENDER

There is confusion about the terms *sex* and *gender*. Unfortunately, these terms are often used interchangeably, without distinction as to their precise meanings. I use the terms sex and gender to distinguish between biology (nature) and identity development (nurture).

Sex

Sex refers to anatomical maleness and femaleness, the biological developments that happen to us before birth, or the "nature" side of our being. Most animal species are differentiated by sex. The sex of a child is revealed at birth—or earlier, through amniocentesis or sonography.

"It's a boy!" or "It's a girl!"—the proclamation of the sex of a child—is usually the first description the child gets. Parents used to have to wait for the birth to know what sex their child would be. Now, through advances in medical technology, they can learn of the sex many months before the birth and can begin to prepare for the socialization of their child based on what they believe the sex will be.

Sex is determined by our genes, which trigger hormones to make us grow either male or female genitalia. Some theorists also believe that sex hormones cause differences in the brain and central nervous system as well. Sex cannot be changed, at least not the genetic aspects of sex. Even though a few people have undergone hormonal treatment and surgical procedures to change the anatomical aspects of their sexual being, their genetic programming stays the same as it was at the time of birth.

Gender

Gender, by contrast, is a term that is uniquely human. Gender describes masculine and feminine identity, the environmental or cultural developments that begin to happen to us at our birth or even before. This is the "nurture" side of our being.

"We'll name her Mary," or "We'll name him John," is the designation of gender. "I bought Mary a pretty pink dress with ruffles," or "Look at this cute cowboy outfit for John," furthers the labeling of gender. What we name our children, how we dress them, how we decorate the nursery—all add to the gender-imprinting of a new child.

There are books that provide lists of potential names for boys or for girls. Clothing stores are filled with sections of attire for boys and men and different sections for girls and women. We learn to be feminine or masculine from the role models around us (mothers, fathers, sisters, brothers) and from the responses (smiles or frowns) we get when we behave in certain ways (tough or tender).

Boys are rewarded for being strong, for being independent, for being active. Girls are rewarded for being dainty, for being caring, for being quiet. Baby boys and girls are handled differently by parents and others who hold and play with them. From birth, boys are treated in a more boisterous manner and girls are cuddled and protected more. As we grow and develop, we are constantly judged masculine or feminine, based on the observations of others about the way we act, feel, think, and live our lives.

> "I don't know when she is ever going to act like a girl," Cindy's grand-mother moans. "She refuses to wear a dress and insists on playing ball with the boys."
>
> "Smile, girls, smile," urges the cheerleader coach for the third-grade girls. The girls are giggling and cheering the boys on to win on the football field.
>
> "He's a sissy. He's a scaredy-cat. He's a wimp," are the fighting words that little boys live in fear of.

While sex is typically determined at or before birth, gender is more pliable and varied. Gender characteristics develop and change over the life span. Some boys and men adopt an array of so-called feminine behaviors and attitudes and some girls and women have incorporated so-called masculine behaviors and attitudes into their lifestyles. Ide-ally, we all have various combinations of both masculine and femi-nine traits, which develop, change, and grow throughout our lives. Some gerontologists believe that women and men grow to be more alike in late life because their gender characteristics become more like those of the opposite sex. For example, they maintain, women often become more independent and assertive with age, while men become more passive and relational. By very old age, if these views hold true, men and women are much more alike than they are different.

BIOLOGICAL INFLUENCES ON LONGEVITY

There appear to be at least three biological dimensions that point to natural advantages for females. These dimensions are the genetic advantages to females of having two X chromosomes; the relative influences of sex hormones, which are linked to the major causes of death; and the advantages of being a "pear-shaped" female rather than an "apple-shaped" male in later life.

Chromosomes

Except for our reproductive organs, men and women have essentially the same body parts—arms, legs, heads, hands, feet, eyes, noses, mouths. We suffer from the same ailments—heart disease, cancer, infections, accidents, mental health disorders. All of our chromosomes are alike except for one pair, and that is the pair that determines our sex. It is the XX and XY chromosome pairing that sets us apart as females and males, respectively.

Surprisingly, we know very little about how that one difference, the Y chromosome, influences longevity. Scientists believe that females have an advantage in having two X chromosomes to rely on throughout life, because the second X chromosome provides a backup if something goes wrong with a gene on the first one. If there is a defective gene on one X chromosome, the matching gene on the other X chromosome—which may be unflawed—will override the defective one. This phenomenon in the female is called the *X-inactivation process* or *mosaicism*. Although the female advantage was described many years ago by Ashley Montague in *The Natural Superiority of Women*, only recently has scientific evidence been able to substantiate Montague's theory.

Other than the genetic codes to stimulate the production of male hormones, little is known about the function or benefits of the Y chromosome. Dr. Kirby Smith of Johns Hopkins University has been conducting research on a group of Amish men, who tend to outlive their wives. He has discovered that these men have one arm of the Y chromosome missing, and other authors have speculated such findings might mean that the Y chromosome has detrimental effects on longevity. However, Dr. Kirby has not yet published his findings and cautions against premature statements because his research has not yet ruled out other factors that might be contributing to the longevity of these men.

Hemophilia is an example of the sex-linked diseases that afflict males in much greater proportion than females as a result of these XX and XY processes. The recessive gene for hemophilia is carried on the X chromosome, so if a female has one gene for hemophilia, she is less likely to display symptoms of the disease than a male—chances are that she has a healthy gene on the other X chromosome to override that troubled gene. By contrast, a male who has the recessive gene will not have such protection and will develop the condition.

Fortunately, most diseases seem to result from a combination of genetic factors intertwined with environmental factors. This means that even though we may have genetic vulnerability for a certain disease, we are often able to avoid that disease by controlling our environment and our behaviors so that the defective genetic programming is not activated.

> "Since my dad died early from heart problems and his father also died of heart disease, I know that I have to be careful to protect myself," says fifty-six-year-old Beatrice. "My mother has lived a lot longer than my dad and I hope that I take more after her, but you never know, so I watch my diet and try to get as much exercise as possible. I gave up smoking years ago and get regular checkups to stay on top of any health problems that may develop."

Because the genetic factors that influence the immune system are carried on the X chromosome, there also seems to be a biological basis for women's greater resistance to infectious disease. Although research on sex differences in immunology is sparse, there is some evidence that females may have stronger immune systems than males. However, this blessing turns into a curse for some women. When the immune system is especially sensitive to threats of disease, it can sometimes go awry and begin attacking cells in one's own body. The results of such a disorder of the immune system are autoimmune diseases like multiple sclerosis, rheumatoid arthritis, lupus, and fibromyalgia, which strike women more often than men. Along with osteoporosis, these diseases compromise the quality of life for many older women.

> Beatrice continues, "My mother has developed rheumatoid arthritis and I expect that I will end up with that too. I don't know how to prevent something like that. I just hope that they find a cure or better treatment for it before I reach my mother's age so I don't become incapacitated like she is."

Hormones

A more promising way to study sex differences in longevity has been to look at the major causes of death and try to determine what advantages females have and what disadvantages males have in regard to these risk factors. At the turn of the century, tuberculosis was the major cause of death in this country, and throughout the years smallpox, diphtheria, polio, and other infectious diseases have taken their toll on our population. Now that we have achieved control of those diseases, they are no longer the serious threats they once were, and many more women are surviving to benefit from the natural advantages of their sex and gender in old age.

At the close of this century, the leading causes of death, ranked from highest to lowest, are as follows:

1. Heart disease
2. Cancer (all types)
3. Cerebrovascular diseases (strokes)
4. Accidents (especially motor vehicle accidents)
5. Chronic obstructive pulmonary disease (respiratory illnesses)
6. Pneumonia and influenza
7. Diabetes
8. Cirrhosis of the liver
9. Atherosclerosis (blockage of the arteries)
10. Suicide
11. Homicide
12. Disorders in infancy

Males die of all these causes at greater rates than females, and there are significant sex differences in at least five categories: heart disease, cancer, accidents, suicide, and homicide. In addition to these leading causes of death, other diseases such as AIDS also take the lives of more men than women. Hormones have much influence on both the biological and the cultural factors involved in these causes of death.

ESTROGEN Medical scientists believe that premenopausal women enjoy a buffering effect from illness because of the female sex hormone *estrogen*. Estrogen is believed to protect women against heart disease and osteoporosis. Recent studies are also pointing to the beneficial effects of estrogen on prevention of organic brain disorders such as Alzheimer's disease.

Dr. William R. Hazzard of the Bowman Gray School of Medicine at Wake Forest University is the leading authority on the biological aspects of the sex differential in longevity. He believes that the greater longevity of females appears to have a fundamental biological basis that is not yet fully understood. It seems clear that estrogen does give women an advantage over men until menopause, when women discontinue production of natural estrogen. However, with the advent of hormone replacement for women after menopause, women may increase the effects of this hormonal buffering against heart disease for many years after their bodies have ceased to produce estrogen naturally. If this proves to be true, then the gender gap in longevity could increase as hormone replacement therapy becomes more prevalent among postmenopausal women.

There is still much concern about possible side effects of hormone replacement for women, especially about increased risks of cancer. We do not yet know if the risks will outweigh the benefits toward increasing longevity for women. Surprisingly, even though estrogen replacement is now being strongly promoted as a means of preventing cardiovascular disease in old age for women by the medical and the drug industries, little investigation has been done on whether estrogen treatment might benefit men.

> "It's hard to know what to do about estrogen replacement," worries Beatrice. "Since the men in my family have had serious heart problems, I think that maybe I should take estrogen now that I'm past menopause, but I worry about breast cancer. Plus, I resent the way the drug companies are pushing this so hard without good research on what it may do to our health years down the road."

TESTOSTERONE   The Y chromosome is important in that it triggers the activation of the male sex hormone *testosterone* early in fetal development. When testosterone washes over the embryonic brain, it is believed to cause significant sex differences in brain and central nervous system development and functioning. While this genetic theory of sex differences in mental and psychological development provides interesting areas for research and speculation, the contribution of the Y chromosome to the issue of longevity cannot be determined at this time.

There is good evidence, however, that testosterone is related to increased activity, impulsiveness, irritability, and aggressiveness. These factors are suspected of creating health-related problems for men. Dr. Cheryl Brown Travis, in her book *Women and Health Psychology: Biomedical Issues*, states, "The mere presence of testosterone seems to elevate the body's response to many stressors (for example adrenaline), whereas the presence of estrogens tends to ameliorate stress responses." In a footnote, she comments, "The humorous remark that men are victims of testosterone poisoning is not without basis in fact" (p. 16).

Effects of testosterone on the central nervous system are believed to be the source of many of the aggressive, risk-taking behaviors seen in some boys and men. James Dabbs and Robin Morris at Georgia State University have conducted a large-scale study of U.S. military veterans. They found that those with very high levels of testosterone were much more prone to engage in antisocial behaviors; to have more difficulty with parents, teachers, and classmates; to engage in assaultive behavior; to go AWOL from military service; and to use drugs and alcohol.

These researchers also found, however, that those men with high levels of testosterone who also had higher incomes and education were less apt to engage in illegal or violent behaviors than those with lower incomes and education. They conclude, "Individuals high in SES [socioeconomic status] tend to avoid individual confrontations, especially physical ones, and to submit to years of schooling. Perhaps the antisocial behavior associated with high testosterone interferes with education, but those individuals who do become highly educated are better equipped to control their antisocial tendencies" (p. 211). They point out that those with money and education can take out their aggressions in more socially sanctioned ways, such as driving fast in race cars rather than stealing cars, or playing college football rather than attacking each other in street gangs.

In ancient times, soldiers were fed the testicles of animals before they went into battle to increase their ferociousness and aggression. In modern times, men are injected with male hormones to treat sexual impotence. The political right periodically calls for castration or aversive drug treatment as punishment for male sex offenders. "It is the only way our citizens can be safe from these sex-crazed criminals," is the cry of such politicians. While male assaults on women are serious concerns in our society, male assaults on themselves or other men are a major threat to the longevity of men. Of the twelve leading causes of death, at least three are attributable to aggressive or risk-taking behaviors: accidents, suicide, and homicide. Men are three times as likely to die from accidents (including motor vehicle accidents), more than five times as likely to die from suicide, and more than four times as likely to die from homicide than are women.

Are men's assaultive behaviors a result of excessive amounts of testosterone leading to dangerous aggressive behavior—or does aggressive behavior stimulate the production of testosterone? Which comes first, the chicken or the egg?—or in this case, the testosterone or the aggression? The research is not clear. Eleven-year-old Randy (mentioned in Chapter One) shows signs of high levels of testosterone in his physical appearance and the early onset of puberty, but it is unclear whether he gets into fights as a result of high testosterone levels or whether his testosterone levels increase because he makes himself "get real mad" so that he can fight without feeling pain.

Until this hormone-behavior interaction is better understood, we do not know whether it's best to treat men's aggression by behavioral intervention so that testosterone levels do not escalate, or whether testosterone levels should be reduced chemically so that aggressive behavior does not occur in the first place. Neither approach to reducing aggression is easily accepted in a society where aggression is valued as sport (football and boxing) and as necessary for success in business. At this time, castration and aversive hormone treatment for men have been advocated only as punishment for violent and aggressive criminal behavior, while hormone treatment for women is viewed as a positive measure for health and longevity.

Hormone Treatment

While it is clear that biological factors do account for some of the sex differences in longevity, it is only in genetic programming that we have no control of our biology. With increased knowledge about hormones, we are learning to compensate for hormone effects on our health. For postmenopausal women, especially, estrogen replacement seems to reduce heart disease, prevent or delay the onset of osteoporosis, and may even help to prevent or slow the progression of organic brain disorders such as Alzheimer's disease. Such advances in hormone manipulation will result in better health and higher quality of life for older women and may even serve to widen the longevity gap further.

Men have not enjoyed any comparable progress in hormone treatment. The possibility of controlling testosterone to reduce aggressive or assaultive behaviors has not been explored. Until research is done and hormone treatment is available for men to reduce destructive behaviors that result in violence, injury, and death, men will not have the options to affect biological influences on longevity that women now have.

Weight Distribution

We have known for a long time that being overweight is not good for our health. One of the first things our doctors have us do when we go in for a medical checkup is to get on the scales. Researchers and medical practitioners have warned us against the consequences of being overweight, but until recently, they did not explore the differences in weight gain between men and women.

A relatively new and interesting area of study finds not only obesity but weight distribution is significant to mortality rates. Men and women tend to accumulate weight at different points in the life span and in distinctive patterns. The Baltimore Longitudinal Study on Aging conducted studies on weight distribution and age with 771 men and 408 women, aged seventeen to ninety-six, from 1979 to 1986. This group of researchers concluded that men achieve peak weight gains during their fifties, while women reach their maximal plateaus in weight a decade later, in their sixties. Women's weight gains typically are in their lower bodies, in the hips, buttocks, and legs, giving women a "pear-shaped" appearance. Men gain weight in their upper bodies and midsections, giving them a more "apple-shaped" appearance. This apple-shaped pattern of obesity is now believed to be a strong predictor of increased hypertension, diabetes, coronary heart disease, and stroke, diseases that are often lethal. Although this is a relatively new area of research, Reubin Andres from the Gerontology Research Center at the National Institute for Health has concluded, "When fat is distributed primarily in the lower part of the body (hips, buttocks, and thighs), the obesity is relatively benign: associated abnormalities of blood pressure, glucose tolerance, and serum lipid levels may not occur. In contrast, when the fat is distributed intraabdominally or in the neck, shoulder, and arm areas, the obesity takes on a more 'malignant' metabolic prognosis" (p. 852).

DEVELOPMENTAL INFLUENCES ON LONGEVITY

Genetics and biology play important roles in determining when and how we die. The biological differences in men and women account for a portion of the gender gap in longevity, but our behaviors, environments, and personality factors are even more important because these are things that are under our control. We may not be able to change the genetic programming that we inherit—but we can change the amount of stress we endure, the habits we develop, the environments in which we live, and the way we teach our children.

Identity Development

Established theories of identity development have us believe that we must become separated from others in order to find ourselves. Much of popular psychology now entreats us to avoid dependence on others. Sometimes I despair that the only way that our modern culture considers us mentally healthy is if we have no intimate relationships at all—in fear of becoming codependent or too close to someone else. It is not surprising that this view has evolved from a society that emphasizes the superiority of male behavior over female behavior.

Boys are taught to separate from others early in life. Little boys are discouraged from becoming too attached to their mothers and they are encouraged to bond with their fathers through roughhouse play rather than cuddling and showing affection. Girls are allowed and even expected to stay closer to home and family attachments. Little boys are forced to be "strong," to repress emotions, and to deny feelings. Little girls are expected to be softer, more expressive of tender feelings, and reliant on others for help. I see examples of this in my own family all the time.

> Once I was surprised to see my grandson with his best friend, shortly after they had a disagreement and a fist fight. When I questioned them about how they had resolved their anger at each other, they said, "We just started shooting baskets together." They looked at me in disgust and disbelief when I suggested that it might be a good idea to talk about their disagreement now that they had cooled off.
>
> My six-year-old granddaughter, however, talks about feelings constantly. At the same time her brother was engaged in physical aggression and physical play with his friend, she also was in an argument with her best friend. These little girls got mad at each other, argued and then stormed off, vowing never to be friends again. Later, my granddaughter regretted this decision and called her friend on the phone to make up. She began the conversation with the statement, "You really hurt my feelings!" These girls could not imagine that they would want to hurt each other physically. They did it with words and they were not ready to play together again until the air was cleared by acknowledging their feelings and talking about their differences.

As a teenager, I remember sitting by the phone hoping that some boy would call to ask me for a date. Though I hated to be waiting and wondering if he liked me, I always felt that it must be awful to be a boy who had to put his neck on the line every time he asked a girl out because if she didn't like him, he must feel rejected and humiliated. I never knew if boys really felt this way but I suspect that sensitive boys, who had not toughened up to deny their hurt feelings, did suffer greatly from the roles that they were expected to fulfill in the dating period of their lives.

In spite of these cultural expectations, which force sex role differentiation, most psychological theories of identity development have proclaimed male patterns of development as the normal and desirable way to grow and develop for both sexes. Autonomy, separation, and self-reliance are considered psychologically healthy.

Psychological theorists have viewed female patterns of development as immature or undesirable. Attachment, connectedness, and dependence are considered problems. Much of mental health treatment focuses on the need for women to become more independent, individuated, and less influenced by parents, children, and friends. Only lip service is paid to mental health treatment for men to become more dependent, attached, and accommodating to the needs and desires of other people. When men do show these behaviors they are often labeled, like women, as codependent. I often see this attitude in my students, who have learned this label from popular psychology books rather than from developing an understanding of long-term complementary relationships.

"They are very codependent," states the young beginning counselor about a seventy-year-old couple. The wife was ill in the hospital and the husband drove long distances to be with her every day. He refused to attend to his usual chores because he needed to be with her and she wanted him to be at her side. This was taking a toll on his health and his finances, so the counselor viewed it as very dependent behavior. "I don't know what to do to get him to see that he should not be neglecting himself and his affairs," the counselor worried. Rather than seeing this kind of devotion as a strength of the couple, her training has led her to view any attachment as disordered and problematic. However, if the situation were the other way around, with the husband ill and the wife at his bedside, she would probably view that as appropriate and not question it in the same way.

Self-in-Relation Identity Development

Many women have begun to question the traditional views of psychological health that promote autonomy and independence as the only pattern for healthy and normal development. Dr. Jean Baker Miller and her colleagues at Wellesley have described an alternative theory they call the "self-in-relation" model of development for women. They propose that feminine patterns of attachment and relationships are valid and healthy ways to develop and that one does not have to separate from others to discover identity. Indeed, for many, the best way to know oneself is to be in relationship to others.

In an effort to explore this theory of self-in-relation identity development, I often use an exercise at the beginning of my graduate classes in which I ask each student to draw a picture of "the true you . . . the way you are when you are at the peak of well-being." I then ask them to write a descriptive paragraph on the back of their pictures. I use the exercise as a means for students to introduce themselves to each other. I have been amazed at how many women draw others in their pictures and how many men draw themselves alone. One of my doctoral students became intrigued with the self-in-relation model of development and used my exercise in a research study with a hundred college-age students. Just as I had informally observed in my classes, she found significant differences between the males and females in depicting themselves at the height of their well-being. The men much more often drew pictures of themselves alone and the women drew others in their pictures with whom they have meaningful relationships.

In my experience, those people who can be autonomous when it is called for but who can also be dependent when needed without losing their dignity or self-esteem are the people who survive and live well as they grow older. People who build interdependent relationships have the support they need to live alone without being lonely, to get assistance when they need it, and to have meaningful, reciprocal friendships. These things are extremely important for survival.

AN INTEGRATIVE PERSPECTIVE ON LONGEVITY

The argument of whether we live long because of biological factors or because of environmental, behavioral, and developmental factors is outdated and unproductive. We need to integrate the science of nature with the art of nurture to live long and well. As complex, intelligent human beings, we have the capacity to improve on biology, to control, mold, and adapt our behaviors and environments. Biology is important to longevity—but as we understand more about the nature of health and wellness, we know that behavior is the area that is of extreme importance to living long and well. Women may have some natural advantages over men, but surely men can use their intelligence to wake up and change the behaviors that are killing them off prematurely.

Health and longevity depend on much more than physical well-being. By taking a holistic view of our lives, we can begin to identify other life dimensions in which we have strengths and problems contributing to the length of life—and the meaning and quality of life as well.

CHAPTER THREE

Health and Wellness:
Taking Care of Ourselves

W here your health is concerned, do you leave your fate to Lady Luck, do you only fix broken parts as needed, or do you tend to your well-being regularly and try to prevent disease and disability? People usually approach health in one of these three ways, as gamblers, mechanics, or gardeners.

APPROACHES TOWARD HEALTH

Currently, the health news tends to focus on "managed care" issues. The main health debate centers on what health care professionals should be doing and what insurance companies should pay for.

The current health care crisis has not addressed the various ways in which individuals manage their own health care. Yet individual approaches to health care are undoubtedly most important in understanding health outcomes and longevity. The person who relies entirely on physicians and takes no responsibility for his or her own health will have very different health experiences from the person who learns about and understands the dynamics of holistic health and well-being. The outcomes for the person who ignores symptoms and waits until it is too late for treatment are different from the outcomes for the hypochondriac who imagines symptoms that do not exist, and both differ from the health outcomes for someone who takes personal responsibility for his or her own well-being. For these reasons, health and wellness depend less on health care professionals and systems than on individual approaches to health care.

Health Gamblers

Gamblers trust genes, God, and Lady Luck. Shrugging their shoulders, they say, "It's in the genes so it doesn't really matter what I do," or "It's up to God, and he will take care of me." Gamblers believe that they can live their lives in any way they want because no matter what they do, when their time is up, that's it. It's all predestined.

Here are two examples of health gamblers who have trusted their lives to fate.

Though eighty-one-year-old Dorothy would never describe herself as a gambler—she is a very religious person who disapproves of gambling—she had not been to a doctor or taken so much as an aspirin for more than fifty years, since the birth of her younger daughter. She believed that God had a plan for her and when it was her time to die, the Lord would take her. This approach to health care worked well for her until she began to suffer terribly from rheumatoid arthritis and depression after the deaths of several friends and family members.

She resisted the idea of seeking professional help, but her daughters finally persuaded her to go for a geriatric assessment at a community health clinic. There the doctors told her what she already knew, that she was depressed and had arthritis, but this evaluation was the first step in breaking her resistance to seeking health care. Now she goes for regular checkups but continues to refuse any invasive medical procedures, such as a biopsy of a lump in her breast that was discovered on a mammogram. She continues to feel that her life is in the hands of the Lord.

For the most part, Dorothy has gambled and won. She has lived longer than the average life expectancy, and the breast lump on her first mammogram did not show up on a following mammogram six months later. She continues to distrust the medical system and only agrees to use it if it brings her some relief from pain.

—⁓—

Henry was a gambler who died at age fifty-seven. He was a successful salesman for a pharmaceutical company, and knew all about drugs and medical treatments. Though he was part of the health care profession, he didn't trust doctors and scoffed at traditional treatments. He had a gregarious personality and was always ready to try the latest health fad and to give his own brand of health advice to the many friends and acquaintances who trusted him.

Henry was a heavy smoker and grossly overweight. He tried to lose weight with the drinking man's diet, the high carbohydrate diet, the grapefruit diet, or whatever was featured in the latest magazine, but he loved smoking and never seriously thought about giving up cigarettes.

At age forty-five, Henry developed a hacking cough that wouldn't go away. Finally, when he started coughing up blood, his wife forced him to see her doctor. The doctor diagnosed lung cancer and scheduled Henry for surgery. After that, Henry gave up smoking and spent the remaining years of his life in search of the ultimate nonmedical cure. He traveled around trying one nontraditional treatment after another, and always had great hope with each new treatment. His cancer went into remission for several years, then recurred. He finally died twelve years after he was first diagnosed with cancer.

His approach to health care remained that of a gambler to the end. He played the health care market as he might have played the lottery, buying alternative cures as though they were lottery tickets. Like a confirmed lottery player, he was convinced that he would win the prize if only he bought enough tickets, and he had no more interest in traditional medicine than a lottery player has in building secure assets by banking or investing money in traditional ways.

Health gamblers who live into old age are the exceptions and undoubtedly have very good genes and immune systems to survive so long. Some attribute their fate to God or to clean living, but can't explain why their friends and family who have led similar lives have died at earlier ages. Most people who abuse their bodies with cigarettes, drugs, alcohol, and food and who ignore or deny treatment for their health problems do not live to see old age.

Health Mechanics

Unlike gamblers, health mechanics take care of their health as needed. Health mechanics view health much in the way they view the maintenance of their cars. If it's running all right, then there's no need to fix it. If it's broken, then you look for the cause and make repairs. They're either do-it-yourselfers who use home remedies when they get sick or good patients who go in for regular checkups to keep everything in good running condition. They get lube jobs (medications, diets, exercise routines) and new parts (teeth, joint replacements, organ transplants) as needed.

It's been my observation that most men (and some women) take a mechanical approach to health. As long as their bodies seem to be functioning okay, they avoid going in for regular checkups and health maintenance. Men win applause for being tough and performing against all odds, even when they have pain or illness. We've all watched football players and other athletes refuse to quit playing when they were in obvious pain after being hit and hurt. Even when these men are sick, they typically rely on their wives or mothers to take care of them. They delay seeking professional treatment, so that by the time they do seek attention, they may be in serious trouble and need more aggressive treatment than would have been necessary if they had sought help earlier. Women often complain that they cannot get their husbands (or their fathers, sons, and brothers) to go to a doctor and that their men keep on working in spite of feeling ill. These men are often better mechanics of their cars than they are of their own health.

Barney sold and installed bottled gas systems for people whose property was not hooked to natural gas lines. He had to be sure that his customers understood proper maintenance and care for these large tanks of explosive material. Unfortunately, he was not so careful about his own health. He smoked heavily from the time he was a teenager until after his first heart attack.

He knew that cigarettes were not good for his health but he felt good and performed well. He saw no reason to go to the doctor for regular checkups and believed that the manual labor of his work and his bowling league activities gave him all the exercise he needed. Even though his father died of a heart attack, he had lived into his seventies, so Barney was not worried yet about dying from his bad health habits.

His first heart attack at age forty-five served as a wake-up call. Barney quit smoking with great struggle, resentment, and feelings of deprivation. He used gum as a substitute for cigarettes and bought Spearmint by the case. It never satisfied him. He began to think seriously about retiring, although he didn't know how he would afford it. He made a couple of visits to Florida and decided that he wanted to retire there where it was warm and the fishing was good. Then he had a second heart attack.

With his second heart attack, Barney lost hope of full recovery and began making active plans to quit work and move to Florida. Before he could accomplish this, however, Barney's mother died. He was devastated. Two weeks later, at age fifty-one, Barney had a third heart attack and died. His cigarette smoking had taken its toll and his attempts to change destructive health habits and to enjoy life more were too late in coming. He had been a better mechanic in his work than he was in his life. Barney died in 1966. Had he been born thirty years later and encountered the same problems today, he would probably be a good candidate for bypass surgery and possibly even a heart transplant, but those approaches to repairing hearts were not yet available when he needed them.

Most of our medical advances and treatment are based on a mechanical approach to health care. People who take advantage of this modern-day system can now expect to keep their bodies functioning for a long time by regular maintenance and repair. This is the approach that has enabled us to extend life expectancies so dramatically in this century. However, we are complex organisms and not machines, and modern medicine still does not know how to treat or address some of the chronic health problems that plague the lives of many people.

Hypochondriacs

Some people (especially women) get labeled hypochondriacs because they have such vague complaints that their physician cannot determine what is wrong or how to treat them. As a result, they often end up incorrectly diagnosed and treated and often overmedicated. They worry over their health so much that they never feel entirely well.

Barney's second wife, Hilda, was a hypochondriac. She had been to consult every doctor in the small town where they lived. She insisted on being admitted to the hospital for diagnostic tests whenever the physician could not give her a specific diagnosis for the pain she was feeling. One nurse in the hospital revealed that Hilda's physician had ordered the nursing staff to keep all reading materials away from her during her stay because she would develop the symptoms of whatever disease was highlighted in the current *Reader's Digest* or *Woman's Day* magazine. In spite of her constant health complaints, no serious illness was ever diagnosed during her youth and middle age.

After Barney's death, Hilda moved to Florida where they had planned to retire and where she could be close to her only child. The last that I heard about her was that she became an invalid in her old age as a result of a freak accident. I have often wondered if she is more content now that she has become the invalid that she always professed to be. At least, she can now fit into a mechanical approach to treatment because she finally has medically diagnosable problems.

—∽∽—

Rose is another woman labeled as a hypochondriac. At ninety-one, she has lived most of her adult life going to doctors, seeking some answers to her abdominal pain. When her husband died thirty years ago of cancer, Rose retained his home-health nurses to stay on and attend her. Even though she has had several surgeries and numerous and extensive diagnostic examinations, her physicians cannot explain her ailments and usually write them off to depression. Now that she is old, they also say she has organic brain disorder (dementia), even though she shows no symptoms of memory impairment. She has lived in a nursing home for more than ten years and employs a companion to take care of her personal needs in addition to the nursing care the staff provides.

Unlike Barney, this woman has been so obsessed with her health that she makes herself sick. Her constitution is strong, as is her will to find an answer to her pain. Toward that end, she has ordered an autopsy at her death because she is convinced that the cause of her health problems will then be discovered.

Barney, Hilda, and Rose present the issues involved in health care that a mechanistic approach fails to address. It is much more complex to maintain health than to simply find the cause of a specific disease and treat it with medicine or surgery. For genuine well-being, one must avoid destructive habits and the expression of psychological distress through physical complaints, and also work at keeping health problems from being exacerbated by other life issues such as family, environmental, occupational, or spiritual conflicts. As in the three case examples, men die more often than women from these failures in our approach to health care. In addition, though women live longer, many exist with a very poor quality of life because they do not get adequate treatment with current medical models of health.

Health Gardeners

Health gardeners view their health much in the way that they might observe and nurture plants. They pay attention to their environment. They are concerned with proper nutrition and good health habits. They are sensitive to small changes and try to catch problems early so that little things do not develop into life-threatening conditions. Good gardeners attend to their health regularly and appropriately. They consult with others regarding specific health problems and seek help from many sources, including health professionals, reading materials, friends, and their own life experiences. They are sensitive to their own bodies and their own best interests. They use preventive measures, alternative treatments, and traditional health care to prolong their lives and enhance their well-being. They take responsibility for their own health and try to learn as much as they can about how to be better gardeners for their health and the health of others as well. It is my experience that more women than men take a gardening approach to health.

As I said earlier, our society's mechanistic approach has helped us reach the high level of health care that we now enjoy. But human beings are not machines like automobiles; we are living organisms like plants. As such, we need to nurture and care for ourselves and others as gardeners. Health, like life, is a process, not a product that we obtain and keep forever. It is ever changing, constantly in flux. It requires continual attention and monitoring to stay well and live long. It also requires help from formal, informal, and personal resources.

Often when we think of health, we think only of our physical state; but we are complex beings with multidimensional lives involving emotions, occupations, relationships, intellectual abilities, spiritual beliefs, and environmental conditions, as well as our physical well-being.

Meg, a survivor of breast cancer, was introduced in Chapter One. She has learned to be a gardener and to see all aspects of her life as integral to her physical health.

Meg is now five years past surgery for breast cancer. She had a radical mastectomy and two attempts at reconstruction to implant a prosthetic breast, and is considered a cancer survivor. This experience has changed her life.

At age forty-six, she was a successful attorney, a former teacher, a wife and mother of two college-age children. Some would say that she had it all.

Then she found a lump in her breast and was diagnosed with breast cancer. Her life was turned upside down. The first problem was that her husband was not there for her when she needed him most. They had been growing apart for many years. Now, when she needed his love and support, he was not able or willing to give it. She believes that he was so frightened of the possibility of her dying that he avoided dealing with it at all.

A second problem was her stressful work environment. As she began to make life changes, she became more sensitive to environmental conditions, including secondary smoke. Many of her colleagues, including her boss, smoked cigarettes and were not willing to establish a smoke-free office. She would have liked to have found another job but couldn't afford to give up her health insurance coverage, so she had to stay where she was.

A third problem was her religious beliefs. She was active in a church that provided many social benefits but few spiritual supports for understanding the life-and-death issues that she was facing. She had always considered herself to be agnostic, but now it was not enough to say that she didn't know if there was a God or a higher power. She had many spiritual questions that needed answers.

Meg realized that if she was going to make the life changes needed to survive cancer, she had to take her own health care in hand. The issues in her marriage, her work environment, and her religion were not things that her physicians could treat or understand. Like a good gardener, she began to nurture and care for herself.

In addition to following the medical recommendations and changing her diet, she began to live differently. She confronted her husband about their marriage and coaxed him into some marriage counseling. Then she went to the human resources office at her company and pushed for a no-smoking policy. Finally, she sought out spiritual resources and groups that would provide her with the nourishment she needed to accept her illness and her possible death.

These actions resulted in her getting a divorce, obtaining a smoke-free work environment, and finding a new circle of friends in a spiritual community that provides comfort, inspiration, and understanding.

Meg is certain that without these changes, she would not have survived her cancer even with the best medical care in the world. She lives alone but is happier now than she was before her diagnosis. She is no longer a mechanic, going in for checkups and following medical orders; she has become the manager of her own health. As a cancer survivor, she may not be viewed as a healthy person, but she is experiencing a high level of wellness in her life.

Wellness is the garden or context in which we experience health. For example: we may be physically healthy but far from feeling well and happy with our lives. Conversely, we may enjoy a high state of well-being while suffering with a physical illness. This contextual process of multidimensional health and well-being is extremely important to aging and longevity.

A MODEL FOR WELLNESS

To enjoy a long and high-quality life, we must move beyond the simplistic, mechanical ways of dealing with physical health as though our bodies were automobiles needing new parts or headed for the junkyard when they can no longer perform. We must also strengthen and toughen ourselves to endure in a variety of environments and to overcome adversity. We need to be dependent on others when appropriate for care and we need to be self-assured and independent enough to pursue individual answers and management of our own health. To do this, we need a comprehensive understanding of the variety of influences on our health and well-being in our complex lives.

For approximately ten years, the Fisher Institute for Wellness at Ball State University has been concerned with holistic health. My colleagues, Neil Schmottlach, a physical education professor and director of the institute, David Gobble, a health sciences professor and health educator, Donald Nicholas, a counseling psychology professor and health psychologist, and I, a geropsychologist and coordinator of the Center for Gerontology, have worked together to research and better understand life-span wellness. Of course, I have been especially interested in better understanding the gender differences in aging that result in women living longer than men.

Our team has come to think of the human as an organic system rather than as a machine. Over the past several years, we have developed a model for life-span health and wellness that has the following principles:

- *Health is multidimensional.* Holistic health involves many more aspects of life than just physical well-being.
- *Health is dynamic.* Holistic health is never static; it is constantly changing, evolving, and interacting with the environment.
- *Health is self-regulating.* Holistic health is constantly adjusting by means of feedback mechanisms to maintain a balance within each life dimension and between all life dimensions.
- *Wellness is the context* within which this dynamic, adjusting, balancing system of health operates. Holistic health is a process that happens within the context of an integrated state of well-being.

With such a complex, ever-changing system as the human organism, each person has a unique experience with health and wellness. One person may be diagnosed with cancer, lose hope, and die quickly. Another with the same diagnosis may live on for many years but never recover. And a third person may have a full remission and live a long life, dying at last of some other illness. Physicians will readily admit that they do not fully understand what keeps one person alive and kills another when both had the same degree of illness. Our biological responses and our mental interpretations of similar illnesses can be extremely varied.

In the remainder of this chapter, I describe each of these four wellness principles in more detail. However, keep in mind that these principles work together as an integrated system and do not operate independently of each other.

Health Is Multidimensional

Almost everyone would agree that we live very complicated lives that have many aspects or dimensions. One reason most people give for ignoring physical health is that they don't have time to do the things they know they should do to prevent illness and to stay healthy. In our very demanding lives, we have to be concerned with our jobs, families, education, community and church responsibilities, politics, and environment, in addition to eating right, exercising, and getting regular checkups. These are the things that we call life dimensions in our model for wellness. These life dimensions could be divided up in many ways.

Many people are familiar with the three domains of body, mind, and spirit used by the YMCA and other organizations. Researchers and health professionals often divide health into the physiological, sociological, and psychological realms. In our model, however, we have chosen to identify and explore seven life dimensions. These include:

- Physical health
- Emotional health
- Intellectual health
- Social health
- Occupational health
- Spiritual health
- Environmental health

Of course, there are other ways in which our lives might be categorized and some important areas of life may overlap. For example, sexuality is an important part of our health and well-being, but does it belong in the physical, emotional, or social dimensions in this model? Relationships are definitely important in the social dimension, but they are also important to our emotions and occupations. So these dimensions overlap and are not exclusive of one another, but they still provide a framework for exploring our multifaceted lives. In the following chapters on gender differences in longevity and life-span wellness, I organize multidimensional health within this framework and use the following descriptions for these life dimensions:

PHYSICAL HEALTH Physical health is obviously what most people refer to when they talk about health. It describes our physical state. It includes weight, height, sensory modalities (like vision, hearing, taste, touch, smell), body type, skin condition, disease, physical disability, and so on. We may be keenly aware of our bodies or we may be insensitive to them, but most of us could probably identify something about the state of our physical well-being at any given time, if asked to describe how we are feeling. "I feel great!" "I feel like I'm getting a cold." "I feel queasy." "I feel fat." These are all statements about physical health. This domain also includes our attitudes about and relationships with medical professionals and treatment.

EMOTIONAL HEALTH Emotional health depends on our ability to express how we are feeling. Though most of us can describe our physical state, fewer people are able to identify their emotional state of well-being and many attempt to hide or deny their feelings.

While it is generally acceptable to be physically ill in our society, there is a strong stigma on emotional illness and most of us feel embarrassed or ashamed to have feelings other than the ones considered positive and normal by most people. This domain also includes our attitudes and behaviors about mental health treatment.

INTELLECTUAL HEALTH Intellectual health involves our abilities to think, solve problems, learn, and make judgments. Often intelligence is described in terms of IQ or intelligence quotients. IQ tests are measures of how well we can cognitively function in society but research shows they have many flaws and some biases against those who do not conform to the predominant culture. Therefore, intellectual health, here, describes more of an approach to life. Is there a level of curiosity, a desire to learn new things and to know more? Is there the ability to make good judgments and to solve everyday functional problems? Intellectual functioning describes how well we think for ourselves and work to develop our intellect. Included in this dimension are issues of retraining and continuing education throughout life.

SOCIAL HEALTH Our social health refers to our relationships, social activities, and social supports. Sometimes I like to call this dimension relational health, because it includes friendships, families, acquaintances, lovers, and community involvements. How are we related to others? What are our supportive systems? Do we operate alone, autonomously, or within groups? Are we self-reliant or dependent? Where do we get support when we need it? These are all questions that are concerned with our social health. Included in this domain are the important issues of giving and receiving care.

OCCUPATIONAL HEALTH Work is the core of life for most people. It gives us purpose, economic resources, and identity. How do we occupy ourselves vocationally and avocationally? What is our training? What are our hobbies? What are our skills? How much money do we make? How much power do we have? How much stress do we encounter in our occupations, whether as business executives or homemakers? What will it mean to retire? These are some of the important aspects of the occupational influences on our health included in this life dimension.

SPIRITUAL HEALTH Life without meaning is empty. Spiritual health involves our life satisfaction and connection to what came before and what will come after our time on this earth. What gives meaning and purpose to our lives? What do we honor from the past and what do we want to leave for future generations? How do we feel about and approach death? Do we believe and have faith in a higher being? All of these questions influence the way we deal with physical illness, aging, living, and dying. Included in this dimension are not only religious beliefs and practices, but creativity, meditation, and spiritual connectedness through the legacies we leave and our involvement with nature.

ENVIRONMENTAL HEALTH Environmental health is concerned with the space in which we live and breathe and how it affects our overall well-being. This can refer to our homes, offices, communities, nation, or world. It may mean our physical surroundings or it may mean the type of emotional environment that can lead to stress. Do we live in low-stress, nurturing, healthful communities, workplaces, and homes? Are we seeking out and relating to positive, life-affirming people or are we surrounded by people who promote negative, hostile, competitive relationships? While emotional health refers to our internal well-being, environmental health involves our external surroundings. Much of the stress that affects all other aspects of our lives comes from the environmental dimensions of our lives.

Health Is Dynamic and Self-Regulating

Our health is in constant flux. We may feel perfectly okay at one minute and then—as a result of an accident or bad news—we may be in bad shape physically or emotionally the next. We can wake up in the morning feeling great but by the end of the day feel tired, irritable, and downhearted. We might be affected by the weather to such a degree that we function very differently in the sunshine and the rain. Since our environments and circumstances are ever changing, so is our health. The changes in our internal processes and our external surroundings keep our state of well-being in flux.

RESPONSE TO FEEDBACK Because of this ever-changing dynamic, our bodies are continually seeking equilibrium. We respond and adjust to feedback from the outside and from the inside to stay in balance. A rather simplistic way to understand this concept is to think of the thermostat on a furnace. If the air surrounding the thermostat gets too cool, the thermostat turns the heat on. When the air gets too hot, the thermostat turns the heat off. Such a feedback response gauge keeps the room at a comfortable temperature all the time. Similarly, our bodies are designed to be balanced and sensitive to our equilibrium, so when we get tired or hungry, we want to sit down and rest or to eat.

BALANCING THE SYSTEM Health is self-regulating within and between life dimensions. In other words, our physical health is constantly striving for balance (by fighting off colds and infection, keeping warm, and so on), as is our emotional health, social health, occupational health, and the rest. Health is also self-regulating between life dimensions, so that if we become physically ill, our emotional well-being is affected. Our social health plays a big role in our physical and emotional well-being. It's also important to have family and friends to take care of us when we are ill. Our occupational health influences our emotional well-being and all other life dimensions as well.

One visual image that helps me understand such self-regulating properties of health is to think of each life dimension as if it were a part of a suspended mobile. This mobile is constantly moving and turning with every little change in the environment surrounding it. A slight breeze makes the mobile move and adjust itself. A big gust of wind can cause the mobile to move faster and to become momentarily unbalanced—but if everything works as it should, it soon returns to its former state. These dynamic, self-regulating properties of a system striving for equilibrium are key to understanding the holistic approach to health, aging, and longevity that is the perspective of this book.

Wellness Is the Context

Out of this process of multidimensional, ever-changing health emerges an overall state of well-being, or wellness. Health is often thought of as a state in which there is no disease, but wellness is much more than the simple absence of disease. Wellness is the polar opposite of illness. High-level wellness is the result of optimal health processes in all life dimensions, while severe illness is the result of serious or long-term disease processes in all life dimensions.

If we think of these concepts on a continuum, it might look something like this:

SEVERE ILLNESS ←← DISEASE ↔ HEALTH →→ HIGH-LEVEL WELLNESS

As we move away from health toward disease, we become more and more ill. As we move away from disease toward health in a positive direction, we become more and more well.

In a multidimensional model for health, we apply this continuum to each dimension in order to assess our total state of wellness. Disease and illness are the terms used to describe physical health, but in mental health we are more familiar with the terms *dysfunction* or *disorder* rather than disease, as in "dysfunctional relationships" or "mental disorders." However, they carry the same idea and can be used on a similar continuum.

While it is probably impossible to be entirely well along all life dimensions, it is also improbable that we are ever entirely ill. Most people always have some dimensions of life that are moving toward the wellness side of the continuum at the same time some dimensions are moving toward the illness side. The process of health is trying to stay balanced by slowing or stopping the move toward illness in some dimensions while simultaneously encouraging movement toward wellness in the others.

For example, when we become physically sick, we can cope, adjust, and recover much better if we have a good, positive emotional outlook on life and a good support system to help us get well. If we become hopeless and helpless when we are sick, then we'll probably get even sicker. If, however, we are well in other life dimensions, we can compensate for illness in the physical realm. The same would be true if we become depressed over the loss of a loved one. Both the emotional and social dimensions of health would become unbalanced and put us at risk of illness. If we are physically fit, however, and have meaning in our lives from our occupational and spiritual domains, we will recover and find hope again and can ultimately build other relationships to compensate for the loss.

The Dynamic Process

In the dynamic health process, then, we are always moving toward wellness and away from illness or toward illness and away from wellness, even when we have no manifestations of disease or when we appear to be very ill. We are always in the process of either getting well or getting ill in all dimensions of our life. This is why sensitivity, flexibility, and resilience in all dimensions of our lives are extremely important. The person who is mindful of what his or her health status is at all times will be able to make corrections and adjustments and take preventive measures to keep the internal systems moving toward wellness. The person who denies pain, represses emotions, is rigid in relationships, and accepts stress at work as normal or inevitable may be moving toward illness and not even know it until the problems have become severe. By contrast, the person who recognizes when he or she is feeling physically low, expresses emotions, has a variety of relationships, and finds ways to reduce and manage stress is moving toward wellness and will be able to address threats to health and well-being sooner and more efficiently. Ben is an example of someone who moved toward illness after the death of his wife.

Seventy-five-year-old Ben had volunteered for a project to be trained as a counselor in nursing homes. He was retired from a lifelong career as an educator. He had been married for most of his adult life to one woman and had two children who lived in other states. His wife had died three years earlier and he was lost without her. He filled his lonely hours by going to nursing homes every day and visiting with the residents. He would go from room to room and from nursing home to nursing home bringing greetings and sometimes small gifts. He found meaning in this and it gave him a sense of purpose in his life, but he never established any long-term, meaningful relationships with any specific residents or staff. He simply made whirlwind visits that made him feel that he was doing something important for others.

In the volunteer training sessions, Ben revealed bitterness about the lack of support he had received from his children, health professionals, and especially from his church during his wife's illness. This bitterness was eating away at his health and kept him from recovering from his grief over her death. It distanced him from his children, made him reluctant to seek medical treatment for his own health problems, and alienated him from his religion. His negative attitudes about medical treatment also put him at odds with the staff at the nursing homes and made him an unwelcome volunteer. Finally, he was asked not to come to the nursing homes anymore, leaving him without anything to do to fill his lonely days and with even more resentment of others.

Eventually, he became very ill and had to be placed in a nursing home himself. He had alienated most of the people in his life, so he had no one to care for him. His children visited when they could. Unfortunately, they did so more out of obligation than out of concern and love. Ben died a bitter and lonely man, never understanding why his good works had not gained him the satisfaction he desired.

Ben's health processes deteriorated across most life dimensions with the death of his wife. Here is a contrasting example of someone who moved toward wellness with the increasing disability of his wife.

Jim was another seventy-five-year-old male volunteer involved in the same project. He also had worked many years as an educator. He was a well-known professor emeritus of a large university and had been a scientist all his life. His department valued his contributions even after his retirement and continued to provide office space for him to come in at his leisure to stay connected with his profession and his colleagues. He became involved with senior athletics as a master swimmer and competed nationally in swimming meets. He was very masculine, with a gruff appearance and manner that was intimidating to people who did not know him well. He lived with his wife, who had a degenerative disease. She became increasingly disabled and dependent on him and he learned to be a caregiver for the first time in his life.

Like Ben, Jim had long been active in his church. After retirement, he assumed responsibility on a volunteer basis for overseeing the grounds and building maintenance of the church. One day, someone at his church made an announcement to recruit volunteers for the counseling project. Jim called and asked in a very brusque manner about the project. At first the volunteer recruiter thought that he was upset because the project was going to hold training sessions in the church building. When asked if there was a problem, Jim responded, "No, I thought I might sign up!"

Jim became one of the most dedicated volunteers. As a scientist, the basic counseling techniques of listening, suspending judgment, and becoming comfortable with displays of emotion were very new to him. He began to visit with a demented man who was unable to speak, but who would burst into tears and grab Jim around the neck and kiss him on the cheek. At first Jim was unsure about these behaviors and was worried that the man might be making homosexual advances. But he learned to "go with the flow, relax, and remember that the man doesn't know what he's doing." Soon Jim became very attached to this nursing home resident and would take him out for walks and for quiet, male companionship. Jim also established meaningful relationships with several other nursing home residents and became aware that a masculine, male presence is very much needed by both the men and women residents. He initiated and led a men's group every week where the few male residents could meet and discuss their past accomplishments, joys, and concerns. Jim made a real contribution while he also enriched his own life by learning new ways to be masculine and to care about others.

For a man who started the project as a rather gruff, independent athlete and scientist, he soon was accepted by other volunteers and nursing home staff as a person who was willing to learn new skills, adapt to new ideas, and be part of a cooperative group. At one of the training sessions, where the volunteers were expressing some very deep feelings, the group closed by giving each other hugs. Jim surprised everyone by exclaiming, "This is what the world needs more of . . . hugs!"

The flexibility, connectedness, and resilience that Jim showed as he struggled with the changes in his life due to his wife's disability, his caregiving responsibilities, and his own aging represent the improvements that may be made in one's quality of life by moving toward wellness in all life dimensions. The changes that Jim made in his occupational, intellectual, physical, and social health enabled him to cope with the distressing parts of his life much better than ever before. The last time I saw him, he was living his old age in a heightened state of wellness.

Ben and Jim were two men in a large group of women volunteers for this particular project. Most of the women volunteers had experiences similar to Jim's in that their own lives were enhanced as they learned new skills and formed new relationships. At the end of the training sessions, we interviewed each volunteer and found that the changes in the attitudes and the well-being of the volunteer counselors were important, not only to the nursing home residents, but to the lives of the volunteers themselves. Most of the other volunteers, like Jim, reported that learning counseling skills had beneficial effects in dealing with their own problems and the problems of their families and friends. They found new meaning in life by helping others and the training group became an ongoing support group for these older, retired people. They formed meaningful relationships and continued to meet monthly long after the training sessions were completed.

I've observed this change in well-being to be true in other projects that I've conducted over the years. The elders who get involved in learning new skills, in forming new relationships, and in challenging themselves and their ideas report an increasing level of life satisfaction and meaning.

GENDER DIFFERENCES IN WELLNESS

To uncover the answers to why women live longer than men, we must look at all aspects of men's and women's lives. Much of the research on gender differences, aging, and longevity has been focused very narrowly on only one or two life dimensions, usually the physical or biological areas. Little has been done to understand longevity in an integrative, holistic manner by using a multidimensional systems approach that incorporates all life dimensions into one interactive model for wellness.

In the chapters that follow, I take each of the life dimensions in our systems model for wellness and discuss the gender differences that have been discovered through research and clinical observation. From the research I've read and conducted, I've concluded that women more often approach health issues as gardeners and men more often as gamblers and mechanics. Women, as a whole, are more in tune with their bodies, form more reciprocal relationships, have more flexible occupational and sex roles, are more involved with lifelong learning, are more resilient in coping with life stressors, and are more emotionally expressive than men. Men, as a whole, have more financial resources, are more constricted in emotional expression and occupational and sex roles, and are generally more independent and self-sufficient than women.

Which of these factors promote health and longevity and which invite illness and life-threatening disease? There are no easy or simple answers. Gender differences in a systems model for wellness show up in each life dimension, so that they overlap and interact and result in balance that promotes health and longevity or in breakdown that ends in disease, disorder, and death. These are the complex issues addressed in the following pages. By understanding these factors more fully, we can then, as men and women, learn from each other to enjoy long lives and a good old age.

CHAPTER FOUR

Physical Health:

Our Bodies, Our Lives

—⁓— I n a multidimensional systems model for wellness, physical health is a very important component. It plays a significant role not only in longevity but in quality of life. Most health promotion efforts, health research, health training, and medical care focus on the physical aspects of well-being. For that reason, we have made great leaps toward understanding how to stay healthy and how to prolong life. Though we have few options regarding our genes and hormones, we have many choices to make throughout life about our behaviors and attitudes, all of which can promote physical health and ultimately longevity.

While men and women have the same physical ailments for the most part and reap the same benefits from good health practices, there are numerous ways in which our physical health experiences differ. We differ in reproductive health, in health-related behaviors, and in the way we access health services. Men and women think about health in different ways and health professionals treat us differently based on gender.

REPRODUCTIVE HEALTH

The most obvious difference between men and women is in reproductive health. Women's bodies are built to conceive, protect, and nurture offspring and men's bodies are built to impregnate women and perform heavy manual tasks. Human development has evolved around these physical differences so that, throughout history, men and women have been steeped in what psychologist David Gutmann calls the "parental imperative." In other words, men are taught that, as fathers, it is their role to defend the family from threats outside the home and to provide economic resources. Women are taught, as mothers, to protect the family inside the home and to provide nurturance and comfort. One of my friends refers to such sex differences in more graphic terms. She says, "Men are the wallets and women are the baby machines of the family." In any event, men are typically expected to be strong and defended against weakness. Women are expected to be accommodating and resilient when faced with adversity.

Of course, these stereotypes have been changing over the past few decades as women have begun to question the limitations of such rigid sex roles. For all the disadvantages that women have suffered from past stereotypes, however, there are a number of ways that the sex roles have benefited women's longevity and have disadvantaged men.

In Chapter Two, I discuss the ways in which biological sex differences give women some health advantages. These differences in genetics and hormones are things that we have very little control over. In this chapter and those that follow, I focus on the gender differences that are under our control. These differences result from the ways in which we live our lives and from the ways that society's expectations and demands on men and women affect our health and longevity. Most of the diseases that kill us result from lifestyles, attitudes, and behaviors in which there are significant gender differences. We do have control of our behaviors and attitudes and we can change our lifestyles. Women have been actively engaged in making such changes for almost thirty years now. Men can change too from the destructive masculine lifestyles that are killing them, if only they recognize the damage that such behaviors are doing to their longevity.

Puberty

As a little girl and as a teenager, I was taught to believe that a woman's menstrual cycle is a curse, a hassle that women have to put up with and that makes us frail and sickly at "that time of the month." I have always heard women's menstrual periods described in very negative terms, and women have been led to believe that they are somehow unclean, contaminated, and undesirable when they have monthly bleeding. In some cultures, women are ostracized and separated from others at the time of their menstrual periods.

Even in the early feminist movement, there were some who believed that menstruation was a handicap. I can remember when "menstrual extractions" were advocated by feminist health groups and instructions and supplies were available to those who wanted to be free from the hassles of using sanitary pads and tampons every month. (Menstrual extraction was a method of removing the monthly buildup of menstrual blood by inserting a small tube through the cervix into the uterus and attaching it to a vacuum syringe into which the lining of the uterus could be sucked out of a woman's body in minutes, rather than waiting for it to slowly drain out over days.) This rather radical movement never caught on—for many of us it seemed even more of a hassle than enduring a menstrual period. It also had potential to cause infections and other health hazards if not administered skillfully.

While the negatives of the menstrual cycle have been emphasized, little has been noted about the other side of this feminine cycle in which many women report feeling energized, creative, and productive. In fact, most girls and women seem to deal with menstrual cycles effectively and don't let them make much difference in how they live their lives. Since we have to accept the physical changes each month, we can focus on the negatives or we can look at the positives in our menstrual cycles. I have come to believe that women's cyclic biology is more of a blessing than a curse and that we are fortunate to have reproductive systems that keep us tuned into our bodies from a very early age. From the time that girls first get their periods, we're made aware that our bodies go through constant changes and that we feel different physically and emotionally at different times of our cycles.

While a few girls receive little education and are unprepared for menstruation, most girls in modern times learn that body emissions are predictable and, as such, can be prepared for and integrated into their lives. Although most girls don't like the hassle or the embarrassment that menstrual periods can bring, they feel grown up and happy that their bodies are working normally when they first get their periods. Girls who are late in starting their periods often become worried that they aren't like their peers.

Girls talk about their periods with each other and with their mothers. In a study done more than fifteen years ago at Stanford, 97 percent of college women reported that they discuss menstruation with their mothers. More recently, I conducted a study on mother-daughter relationships and found that college-age daughters who report close relationships with their mothers usually report that their mothers have positive attitudes about menstruation. In other words, mothers who feel good about being female and impart that to their daughters have much closer relationships with their daughters than do mothers who have negative reactions to their daughters' menstruation.

Even forty to fifty years ago, girls were beginning to get information at schools and at home about menstruation. Beatrice is a middle-aged woman who felt a special bond with her mother when she first started her period.

Fifty-six-year-old Beatrice remembers the day when she first noticed blood on her panties. She was ten years old. She was not alarmed because her mother had told her about menstruation but she didn't know what to do immediately since she was staying at a friend's house while her mother was at work. She took her panties off and hid them until it was time to go home. When she told her mother what had happened and produced the blood-stained panties, her mother found a sanitary belt and tore up some old rags to use for a pad to catch the blood. It all seemed very weird to Beatrice, but she also felt proud that she was growing up and could now know the secrets of adult women.

Later, when her eight-year-old sister came home, Beatrice twirled around and around to make her skirt fly up so that her sister could see the new sanitary belt and pad. Her sister was shocked, "I'm going to tell Mom what you've got on!" Beatrice declared triumphantly, "Mom already knows. She gave me these things to wear because I've started my period."

Sixty-five-year-old Judy does not remember such openness about the subject of menstruation when she was a girl.

"It was such a mystery and I felt very secretive when I started my period," recalls Judy. "I was not prepared and knew nothing about what was happening to me when I first noticed blood on my underpants. I was scared and worried that I had waited too long to go to the bathroom. For some reason maybe that had caused me to bleed. I washed myself thoroughly and the bleeding stopped, so I thought I everything was okay. Later, I guess my grandmother noticed the blood on my pants when she was doing laundry, because my mother asked me about it. All she told me was that this was part of growing up and she gave me some sanitary pads.

That was when I was twelve years old. It wasn't until the next year, in junior high school, that the subject was addressed in home economics class. A very brave teacher told us about menstruation as part of a unit on grooming and hygiene. There was absolute silence in the room and nobody asked any questions, but later, outside class, the girls started sharing information for the first time."

With the advent of better sex education, more openness in the media, and advertisements for feminine hygiene products, it would be difficult for little girls (or little boys for that matter) today to stay uninformed about the basic uses of sanitary pads and tampons.

Two years ago, when I was taking my eleven-year-old granddaughter on a summer vacation with me, her mother was concerned that she might be on the verge of starting her period. We talked about it together and prepared for it. Her mother was worried because she wouldn't be along to share in this big life event with her only daughter, so she gave me a sealed letter with instructions to give it to my granddaughter should she start her first period on our trip. Happily, I never had to use the letter; mother and daughter were able to celebrate the experience together later, after the vacation was over.

Sadly, boys do not have a comparable experience in dealing with their reproductive growth and development. Most boys are surprised when they begin to have nocturnal emissions (wet dreams) or when they have their first ejaculation. They do not understand what is going on with their bodies. They are embarrassed and try to hide the wet sheets from their mothers, who are usually the ones to notice when they do the laundry. Their buddies and their dads are reluctant to talk about this experience in any meaningful way. Wet dreams are kept quiet and many boys worry if they are normal or think that they have urinated in their sleep. The male experience is solitary and isolating while menstrual periods are accepted as universal and bonding experiences for women.

Women may learn to moan and complain about their physical health, but men learn to keep it under wraps and ignore the significance of it during their growing years. If boys talk about it at all, it is most often in a joking, derisive manner, rather than as a normal body function indicative of growing into manhood. Researchers on the subject of boys' experiences with first ejaculations have described this phenomenon as being surrounded by a "conspiracy of silence." This is just one of the ways that our physical differences become gender differences in approaches to health care.

In an effort to find out more about what boys are learning about physical changes during puberty, I asked several mothers who have boys in elementary school what they tell their sons. Most have not discussed the topic with them, but Sally relayed the following:

> "More information about wet dreams was what our ten-year-old son wanted after we watched the sex education film that they are using in his class. We had already discussed most of the other things with him that were presented in the film but he had never heard about wet dreams before and he was really curious. I was kind of shocked and surprised that they included this topic in the film because when I had visited my daughter's class, wet dreams were not discussed. The boys were informed about menstruation but girls didn't learn anything about ejaculations. I'm glad my husband was there to talk to our son because we had never talked about this before and I'm not sure I know enough about boys' experiences with their first ejaculations to have been very helpful to him. I think girls should be informed about ejaculations as well as boys. Why are we so secretive about this?"

The Teenage Years

From these early experiences of puberty, boys and girls enter their teenage years with different expectations of physical changes, especially in dealing with sexuality. Girls are taught that they must exercise control of their bodies; boys are taught that their bodies will make powerful demands over which they have little control.

With the teenage years, girls begin efforts to mold and shape physical appearance to make themselves attractive to the opposite sex. Diets, makeup, hair styles, and clothing become extremely important for most teenage girls. Yet in spite of all this effort to be attractive and to attract men, girls are then charged with the responsibility of fending off sexual advances from boys. Girls are expected to say, "No!" to boys even if their own desire to respond is great.

Boys, by contrast, learn that their hormones are raging and that it is normal for them to "sow their oats" and try to have sex as often as possible. They aren't expected to control their urges and are led to believe that such effort is at best futile and at worst harmful to their health.

Many years ago, I participated in a sexuality workshop where we were paired off for an exercise in which we were instructed to "talk to our genitals" as though they were a person. I happened to be paired up with a very nice young man in his early twenties and was shocked to hear his frustration and helplessness at trying to control his sexual urges. He expressed anger toward his genitals because they demanded so much of his time and attention. He could not study or pursue other interests very well because sexual thoughts constantly interrupted his concentration. He felt overwhelmed and powerless to do anything about this situation. His only hope seemed to be that he would get some relief as he got older.

This experience has made me wonder how we can teach boys to say "No!" to sexual urges and gain control of their lives. As women, we have decried the way girls have all the responsibility and boys have all the fun. But this young man—who may well be typical—was not having much fun. He desperately needed help in gaining control of his body. Learning sexual responsibility and control is important for the physical health of boys as well as girls. Those who don't learn these important lessons are vulnerable to sexually transmitted diseases and even death. For girls, responsibility and control have always been tied to the fear of pregnancy, but now for both sexes, understanding and controlling sexuality is necessary for survival.

Pregnancy

Like menstruation and sexuality, pregnancy also contributes to women's natural experience of tuning in to physical well-being. The first thought of pregnancy often brings about behavior changes in women, even before conception occurs. Women who want children and are knowledgeable about good health practices will immediately make positive changes in their lifestyle. For example, they may pay closer attention to nutrition, drink more milk, and eat more vegetables. If they have been smoking, they may quit; likewise with drinking alcohol. And women who have not paid much attention to health often begin to do so as soon as they find out they are pregnant. In other words, most prospective or expectant mothers begin to protect their families by improving their own health and there are major health education campaigns encouraging them to do so. Prospective or expectant fathers don't have the same motivation nor do they get the same quality of health promotional attention. While many expectant fathers encourage their partners to take precautions, they may in fact decide to work harder so as to make more money and provide more economic resources for a new family, which brings additional stress. Some fathers feel more isolated and lonely because pregnant partners may not give them undivided attention and support as they once did. With pregnancy, women tune in to their bodies so they can protect their child; men tune out and even ignore their own health so they can be strong for their wives and produce more for their child.

The standing family joke for Jennifer and Mike, now in their fifties, was that Mike ended up sick in bed after the birth of their first child because he couldn't take the stress of the long labor. Meanwhile, Jennifer ended up feeling good after their son was born and was disappointed that Mike didn't feel like celebrating with her and the proud grandparents.

Throughout her pregnancy, eighteen-year-old Jennifer tried to follow her doctor's advice about eating balanced meals, taking vitamins, and getting daily exercise. Although she and her young husband were strapped for cash, they shopped carefully and Jennifer tried to avoid eating the junk foods that they had been used to. While Mike was at work at his construction job and then attending classes in the evening at the university, Jennifer spent her time planning for the baby, keeping house, cooking meals, doing exercises, and going for long walks by herself or with her friends.

Jennifer had never smoked but Mike had taken up cigarettes at age sixteen. During the pregnancy, when Jennifer was preparing for their baby, Mike found that he was smoking more and more as he worried about how to make ends meet for his new family. His older coworkers were smokers so he went along with the norm on the job. He was convinced that smoking and drinking coffee helped him stay alert and awake at night while he was studying for his classes. Smoking became the significant way that he dealt with his mounting stress.

On the night that Jennifer went into labor, Mike, in his anxiety to get to the hospital, forgot to take his usual brand of cigarettes along, so he bought a different brand with menthol (which he rarely smoked) from a vending machine. During the fourteen-hour labor, he smoked so much that by the morning—when Jennifer was feeling much better—Mike had to go home to bed because he was so sick from his stress and from smoking three packs of these menthol cigarettes.

Men like Mike who are good providers for their families and who love their children may miss out on other family events as well. Sometimes it is because they are away at work and miss birthday parties and school events. Or they use alcohol or other destructive habits to handle the problems they feel in their traditional roles as the strong, tough heads of the household. They often do not live long enough to see their children grow up and to enjoy their grandchildren.

Menopause

Just as boys do not have the significant physical markers at puberty that girls have, neither do men have the biological marker that women experience at middle age. Around age fifty, a sudden decline in estrogen leaves most women with significant physical changes that are very recognizable and must be dealt with in some way. Just as girls talk about menstrual periods and learn about their body changes from friends and health professionals, so women learn about their body changes when they experience menopause.

As the baby boomers are entering middle age, there is so much interest in menopause that it is now difficult for any woman to go through it without being deluged with information and pressure to take hormone replacement so as to prevent health problems resulting from estrogen deficiency. Advertisements, seminars, television programs, talk shows all highlight the controversy regarding hormone replacement therapy for women. No longer do women have to broach the subject with their physicians. The physicians and the drug companies offer relief from menopausal symptoms as a matter of course. In fact, it is difficult for a woman to resist medical treatment for this natural life event. Women also encounter pressure from those in the women's health movement who advocate against such treatment, so they feel that they are damned if they do and damned if they don't. They have to keep informed and make their own decisions about what is in the best interest of their own health.

Men, by contrast, get very little information about the changes in their bodies during middle to old age. Their hormones decline gradually, with no sudden, dramatic physical changes. Just as their wet dreams and first ejaculations were not discussed in childhood, their concerns about declining sexual potency or failure to obtain erections are not subjects for discussion. The conspiracy of silence continues and men have very little understanding of what is happening to them. Some people believe that the so-called midlife crisis that many men experience is a result of confusion and fear about sexual and physical changes. The man who leaves his wife and family in search of eternal youth in the arms of a younger woman is a theme that replays itself over and over in real life and in fiction. I wonder what would happen if men felt comfortable in talking about their midlife concerns in real and genuine ways with each other or with mental health profession-als? Perhaps we would see men facing this transitional stage of life in more constructive and creative ways.

Years ago, when menopause was a taboo subject, women had many more psychological problems during this time of life than they appear to have now. Bringing these natural health processes out in the open has been very positive for women's health. It is to be hoped that the same result could occur for men if they would begin to be honest about their concerns, so that they could get support and treatment.

Women from the older generations had very different experiences with menopause than those of us who are now in the midst of it. Dorothy and Alice represent two very different pictures of those ear-lier times.

Eighty-one-year-old Dorothy cannot remember when she had meno-pause. She didn't have time or money to get sick because she had to go to work every day to make ends meet. She worked at a very low-paying job and didn't have any resources to fall back on if she couldn't work. "It wasn't that big of deal, I guess, or I would remember more about it," she says. Dorothy is the woman in Chapter Three who avoided doctors for fifty years and who places all her problems in God's hands.

—⁓—

At the opposite extreme, Alice's menopause hit her like a ton of bricks. Her life had been devoted to her family. Then, after the two oldest were married, the youngest went off to college and she started her menopause. She felt physically ill, but worse than that she lost interest in life. It was then that her doctor began to give her medication for depression. Several times she was admitted to the psychiatric unit at the hospital to get intensive treatment and some relief from her multitude of problems. She always perked up after her hospital stays, but soon after returning home, she would be back in her depression. Sometimes she had attacks during vacations, requiring the family to cancel their plans to get help for her. She became more and more afraid of going places and began to give up her activities so she could stay close to home. Everyone was concerned—but nobody knew what to do for her. Her husband continued to work and his life went on as usual as she became more and more disabled from her depression.

Somehow she endured years of feeling bad and finally began to feel better after her husband retired. Now, at age ninety, she remembers those times only as a dim memory, but knows that they were probably the worst part of her life. "I think younger women now have much better attitudes about middle age and better treatment than was available in my time," she observes.

In all, women's reproductive health requires them to be sensitive to the changes in their bodies in ways that men never learn. Women seek out and obtain more education and discussion about reproductive health concerns. Men's reproductive health concerns remain secretive and isolating. Women are more familiar with and learn more control of their bodies, while many men feel disconnected from and controlled by their bodies. In late life, such early learning experiences can make a difference between finding the resilience to recover from health problems or feeling helpless and hopeless when confronted with problems of impotence or illness.

GENDER DIFFERENCES IN HEALTH HABITS

Our patterns of health behavior have strong impact on longevity and wellness. Do men and women seek help when they need it? Do they educate themselves about good health practices? Do they avoid things that are damaging to health and engage in things that improve health? In answering these questions, we gain insight into some important reasons why women live longer than men.

Help-Seeking Behavior

Health care reports from the National Center for Health Statistics and the Department of Health and Human Services indicate that women receive more formal health treatment and men more informal treatment. In other words, women go to doctors for treatment when they are sick, and men more often get cared for at home by their wives or mothers. As a result, health statistics can lead us to believe that women are sicker than men. Women receive more diagnoses and are prescribed many more medications. Most of the physician visits for women are a result of concerns about weight gain, pregnancy, or other reproductive health issues. These sex differences in health statistics have increased as women have begun to get more professional help with reproductive health.

In earlier times, when the pregnant woman was taken care of by other women (and when women's mortality rate was much higher), men tended to be the ones in the family who were more apt to seek professional treatment. Their newly increased access to professional health care has probably done more to extend women's lives than any other change during this century.

Because women are more tuned in to their bodies, they are apt to notice symptoms sooner than men and will seek treatment earlier for less serious illness and for preventive health care. The downside of this is that a woman whose symptoms are vague and difficult to describe runs the risk of being labeled a hypochondriac or psychosomatic by her physicians.

In a study of the lives of women who are living with chronic disabling conditions like lupus, rheumatoid arthritis, multiple sclerosis, and osteoporosis, I've found that many women spend years of misery and pain before they are accurately diagnosed or even taken seriously by physicians. Some of the women in my study were told that their complaints were all in their imagination and were referred to psychiatrists for treatment. Though these women became depressed, they persisted in seeking answers to their health problems until eventually they were correctly diagnosed and treated.

Eva's experience is typical of the women in this study.

"It took almost seven years before I was diagnosed with lupus," says sixty-five-year-old Eva. "My own doctor just thought I was imagining my symptoms. He told me that this was all just part of menopause and that I just had to give my body time to get adjusted to the changes. I would get so fatigued that I couldn't get out of bed in the morning, so he prescribed antidepressants and told me to get some new hobbies. Finally, he referred me to a psychiatrist because he was convinced that all my complaints were mental.

"After another year and no improvement, I began talking to other women and learned that this was not usual for menopause and my symptoms seemed to be different from depression. I began reading about different diseases and finally decided to go to the medical school for a complete evaluation. The doctors there were not sure what I had, but they didn't discount my complaints the way my own doctor had done. They did a variety of tests over several months to rule out many other diseases. Finally, they decided that I had lupus. They gave me the diagnosis over the telephone on a Friday afternoon. I wasn't sure what it was and the only information I had at home was in an old encyclopedia that said that lupus was a fatal disease. I went through hell that weekend, convinced that I was going to die and not having anyone to talk to about my diagnosis.

"Luckily, I've been able to find more recent information and a great support group of others with lupus. Now, I know that there are effective treatments and that I can live a long time if I take good care of myself and avoid the things that seem to cause flare-ups of my disease."

Fewer men are bothered by such chronic diseases or, if they are, they tend to ignore or discount the symptoms. When it comes to life-threatening diseases such as heart conditions or cancers, however, there seems to be little gender difference in seeking treatment. Men and women both often delay going to get checked out until there are clear symptoms or until there is a significant problem resulting from these disorders. Even then, women are not treated as quickly or as aggressively as men. For example, men are diagnosed and treated for heart disease sooner than women.

Diet and Exercise

Most men and women are aware that good health takes some action on the part of the individual. Even the couch potato is aware that nutritious food and some exercise are needed to stay healthy. However, men and women approach diet and exercise differently.

NUTRITION In pursuit of the ideal body image, almost all women want to lose weight. Most men are either satisfied with their weight or want to gain greater body mass. While women tend to be weight conscious and want to be smaller, men are height conscious and want to be taller and larger. These gender differences in desired body images lead to very different health habits in nutrition and physical activity.

From early childhood, girls learn about food. How to shop for it. How to prepare it. How it affects weight. How to eat it in a ladylike manner. Boys learn very little about the complexities of food. They just learn how to consume it. They eat voraciously, quickly, and with very little knowledge of what is involved to get it on their plates. In almost all studies of gender differences in nutrition, girls and women are found to have much more knowledge about calorie and nutrient content and food preparation. Such obsession with food along with the desire for weight loss leads most girls to restrict their diets and some girls to eating disorders such as anorexia or bulimia. Eating disorders are rare in males. When they do occur, they tend to be with men whose occupations require limited weight, such as jockeys or wrestlers. For the most part, though, women's preoccupation with food seems to have a positive effect on longevity. The knowledge women have about food and its preparation carries over to old age, where women are much more skilled at shopping, planning, and cooking balanced meals than men.

In studies of food consumption, men are found to eat more meat, fat, dairy products, eggs, and high-calorie foods than women. Women eat more fruits, vegetables, whole grains, and low-calorie foods and beverages. Men eat in larger bites and much more quickly than women and their intake and rates of consumption are not affected by companionship at meals. Women eat slower, in smaller bites, and consume less when eating with others, especially if their companions are attractive men. Girls learn feminine ways of eating and boys learn masculine ones. With age, then, as they encounter health and dental problems, men are required to give up many of the foods that they have grown accustomed to and love and to change their eating habits, while women have already been engaging in healthier nutritional lifestyles and do not seem to have so much trouble with dietary changes. Women's concerns around food in late life center on the need to give up cooking and to allow someone else to take over that task when needed.

Bert loved to eat meat and potatoes with all the trimmings. His wife was a good cook and he prided himself on his expertise at tending the barbeque grill throughout the summer, cooking steaks, ribs, chicken, hamburgers, and hot dogs. He regularly ate bacon and eggs for breakfast and always ordered rare prime rib at the country club where he played golf. When he dined out, everyone in the party could count on him to send his steak back to the chef over and over until it was cooked exactly to his liking. He lived to eat and drink.

Although he never smoked, he always drank more alcohol than was good for him and his wife worried about what his eating and drinking habits were doing to his health. Then at age seventy, her fears came true; he had a mild heart attack and ended up with quadruple bypass surgery to fix the clogged veins that had resulted from years of eating a high-fat diet.

Bert was amazed at how much better he felt after the surgery. He had more energy and was able to do more than he had in years. Most of all, he was happy to know that medical technology was able to correct the problems his diet had caused. He was relieved that he could continue to live as he always had, eating and drinking and enjoying life. He now stays in closer touch with his doctor for checkups. Although his doctor wants him to change, he does not see much point in altering his lifestyle when the doctors did such a good job of fixing him up. After all, life wouldn't be worth living if he can't do what he enjoys most.

Bert thinks medical science can make him almost as good as new. He sees no reason to change his lifestyle if it means giving up the pleasures that he has enjoyed for so long. His attitude is that he would rather be dead than follow some dietary plan or restrictive health regimen.

EXERCISE Just as women engage in better nutritional patterns, men engage in more physical activity and exercise. Boys are encouraged to play sports, to lift weights, to do outdoor activities. Exercise is the means of developing the body mass and fitness for competitive sports that men desire. Studies of gender differences in exercise show that males play sports, run, jog, swim, and hike more than women. Women are more apt to walk or take aerobic classes for exercise.

However, these studies rarely if ever take into account the types of physical activity that women engage in from morning until night almost every day, doing housekeeping and child care. In all the studies that I have read regarding gender differences in exercise, I have yet to find one that recognizes these very physical, often strenuous, gender-related tasks as exercise. Even those that include such activities as yard work and gardening as legitimate health activities do not mention housework and child care as physical exercise options. Therefore, I don't believe that we have good evidence of the health effects of exercise on gender differences in longevity. One study has found that though men are much more physically active than women in their younger years, they show steady and significant decrease in that activity in their retirement, while women maintain their activity levels at a lower but constant level throughout life. In exercise, as in nutrition, it seems that women are practicing reasonable health habits in their earlier years that serve them well in old age. It is much more likely that a program of walking or exercise classes will be continued in old age than will participation in competitive sports.

Billy is fifty-five years old and describes himself as a Type A personality. He works hard and goes after anything he does with enthusiasm and drive. Until a year ago, he was a heavy smoker; he was incensed when the company he works for established a no-smoking policy. He protested, he ranted, he raved about the unfairness to smokers and he cursed the establishment every time he had to stand outside in the cold to have his cigarette.

He rarely exercised, using the excuse that he was too busy and that he would do that when he retired and had nothing else to do. Then a friend talked him into playing tennis, just to get out and have a little fun. Amazingly, Billy decided to try it and he liked it. In typical fashion, he made tennis a passion and was scheduling matches several times a week.

With this exercise, he began to realize the toll that cigarettes were taking on his breathing and his energy, so he vowed to quit, threw away his last package, and never looked back. Within two weeks, he began having chest pains on the tennis court and ended up in the hospital, prepped for emergency open heart surgery. Like Bert, Billy was amazed at the difference the surgery made. He felt better than he had in twenty years. But unlike Bert, he now became a true believer in making the necessary lifestyle changes.

Healthy living is Billy's new passion. He is studying everything he can get his hands on about nutrition and exercise. He's the best patient in the cardiac rehabilitation program at the hospital. He pushes himself to increase his time on the exercise machines. He is determined to prove to his doctors that his recovery will not take as long as they predict. He was back at work in only six weeks rather than the three months that the doctors recommended. He is enthusiastic about life and is driven to change everything about his life that caused his health problems.

Bert is an example of the health mechanic. Fix the broken parts when they need it and go in for maintenance as needed thereafter. Billy is more like the health gambler who didn't want to think about his health at all—then, when he had problems, he became determined to beat the odds by covering his bets. It would be much better for both of these men if they could slow down, take stock of their lives, and begin to make the kind of changes that will last a long time.

With their heart surgeries, they have a new lease on life, but with their old health habits, they do not know how to make the changes that will be beneficial. Bert may not be so fortunate the next time he has a heart attack—and without making changes there will undoubtedly be a next time. Billy has the right idea about the changes he needs to make but he is approaching them like another competitive project rather than a new way of life. By making such drastic changes with such high expectations for success, he very well may burn out and give up, feeling discouraged and hopeless.

Cigarette Smoking

Men smoke more cigarettes than women and thus end up cutting their lives short. The older group of people today did not have the health statistics or the research available to them in their younger years to understand how devastating cigarette smoking can be. Social customs did not condone smoking among women, but social customs and effective advertising encouraged men to equate masculinity, attractiveness, strength, and power with smoking. The image of the tough, rugged, handsome Marlboro man held a promise to men that was appealing. The chemicals and the behaviors involved with cigarette smoking also prove to be a way to manage stress that aids men in denying their fears and emotions. If you feel weak, a cigarette will make you feel in control. If you feel down or stressed, the act of lighting up and sucking the smoke into your system slows you down a little bit—while the nicotine gives you a boost.

Of course, as women began to break out of the social constrictions of the past, the advertisements for cigarettes were soon targeted to women as well as men. "You've come a long way, baby!" was the slogan that linked the freedom to smoke cigarettes to the women's movement for equality. However, though many women succumbed to such images and the desire to be equal to men in all ways, women have not yet bought into such destructive health habits in numbers equal to men. It's worrisome though that more women are smoking now than in the past.

Lung cancer, which has been directly linked to cigarette smoking, is the number one cancer killer. In 1993, ninety-three thousand men died of lung cancer. A seventy-five-year-old smoker is thirty-three times more likely to die of lung cancer than a seventy-five-year-old man who has never smoked. Many health researchers have noted that men's longevity could be enhanced by several years if men would give up this one destructive habit.

Alcohol and Drug Use

Though women are prescribed more medications and use more over-the-counter drugs, men far exceed women in use of alcoholic beverages and illegal drugs. Men of all ages from twelve on up are estimated to experiment with illegal drugs about 50 percent more often than women. Men use these drugs more frequently and are much more prone to use the more dangerous and addictive drugs at even greater rates.

For example, in a 1993 report by the Public Health Service of the U.S. Department of Health and Human Services, 39.2 percent (38,974,000) of men and 28.7 percent (30,949,000) of women are estimated to have ever tried marijuana, but it is estimated that in the last month of the survey, 6 percent (5,977,000) of men and only 2.8 percent (3,015,000) of women had used marijuana. With the more dangerous and addictive drugs, crack cocaine, 2.6 percent (2,576,000) of men and only 1.1 percent (1,173,000) of women were estimated to have ever tried it, a difference of more than two to one. And in the last month of the study, 0.3 percent (308,000) of men and 0.1 percent (109,000) of women were estimated to have used crack cocaine, a difference of three to one.

Men also exceed women in their use of alcohol. In the 1993 survey, 71.7 percent (71,216,000) of men and 61.4 percent (66,556,000) of women were estimated to have used alcohol in the past year. But 31.2 percent of men and only 12.2 percent of women were estimated to have used alcohol once a week or more during the past year. Over twice as many men as women die of cirrhosis of the liver, a disease that is strongly related to alcohol abuse.

In a 1994 report by the National Institutes of Health, men were found to dominate the mortality, emergency, and treatment admissions for abuse of cocaine, heroin, and other illicit drugs. For example, in San Diego, males accounted for 86 percent of all heroin deaths, in New York City it was 81 percent, and in San Francisco it was 83 percent. In other words, the abuse of drugs is lethal for abusers—and most of the abusers are male.

Health Risk Behaviors

The third leading cause of death that shows significant sex differences is accidents. Men are three times as likely as women to die from accidents.The largest group of deaths related to accidents involve motor vehicles. Many of these accidents also involve alcohol use. Men drive more often, faster, and with less use of seat belts than women do and men use alcohol and other mind-altering substances more than women do, so it is unsurprising that they are more likely to have accidents, especially fatal accidents. In addition to motor vehicle accidents, men experience more work-related accidents. The most hazardous jobs in our society are predominantly occupied by males.

Many more men than women have been placed at risk of losing their lives in defense of the country. As I have worked with and interviewed men in very old age, I have been struck by the fact that very few of them were ever in combat in the armed services. Most were too young for World War I and too old for World War II, or they had deferments. These deferments—exemptions from the draft—were due to physical problems that caused men to be declared unfit for service or to jobs in factories or at universities that were declared important for national security.

The wars of this century have taken the lives of many young men who never had the chance to grow old in the safety of their own communities. The disturbing problem now is that our communities are no longer safe places in which to grow old.

If the first half of the twentieth century was marked by the two world wars that took the lives of many men, the end of the century is marked by wars on the streets of our own country—wars that are still taking the lives of many more males than females. Today, violence in the United States is killing almost four times as many males as females. Men are more often the victims of the gang wars, drive-by shootings, and violence in the drug trade and organized crime. Homicide is one of the leading causes of death for men today. The violence that men do to each other far exceeds the violence that men do to women, yet men do not seem to be as outraged by these trends as women are. Men's violence to women is a horrible blight on our society and women are banding together and demanding action to stop such crimes. Why then do men not recognize the damage that the escalation of societal violence is doing to them as well and work together with women to find solutions?

PHYSICAL HEALTH AND LONGEVITY

Women live longer because they are more in tune with their bodies, seek more professional help, practice more preventive health measures, engage in less destructive health behaviors, and take less risk. Men are more at risk of early death because they are taught to ignore weakness, illness, and health concerns. They not only don't listen to their bodies but they are applauded for the denial of pain and discomfort. They abuse substances and expose themselves to greater hazards in defending themselves and others in times of peril. Though women often suffer more illness and receive more medication and treatment, women manage to survive through their younger years because they take better care of themselves, reduce their health risks, and endure into old age in spite of the illness and sexual discrimination that they encounter along the way.

The few men who survive into old age are often in better physical condition than the women of the same age. Among the very old, gender differences seem to disappear so that very old men and women are much more alike than they are different. Many of these men have become caregivers to disabled wives. They have found ways to take care of themselves and others. They pay attention to their health and seek help from their doctors and other health professionals in equal numbers to women. These men are exceptional and should provide excellent role models for younger men about lifestyles, attitudes, and behaviors that have enabled them to live so much longer than most of their peers. We need to learn more about these very old men to determine what true masculinity can be and how it can work to protect men rather than to destroy them.

CHAPTER FIVE

Mental Health:

Our Minds, Ourselves

P hysical health is greatly influenced by mental health, and vice versa. So much so, that in the multidimensional systems model for wellness described in Chapter Three, the interactions among the physical, emotional, and intellectual dimensions of life become vitally important to living long and well. Our emotions and thought processes have been proven to affect disease processes both positively and negatively. So whether we have good or poor health depends not only on genetic programming, hormonal influences, medical conditions, and health behaviors, but also on our beliefs, attitudes, and emotional states.

Mental health includes at least two life dimensions, emotional well-being and intellectual knowledge, beliefs, and attitudes. Gender differences in emotional and intellectual dimensions of life cast additional light on why men are not surviving into old age at rates equal to women. Men and women have different styles of emotional expressiveness, stress management, communication, and lifelong learning. Some of these differences have lethal consequences, resulting in more deaths of men than women at each stage of the life span.

EMOTIONAL EXPRESSION

When it comes to emotions, men need solvent; women need glue. That is the belief of a psychotherapist friend of mine. What she means by that statement is that men who come for therapy often have their emotions buried deep within so that they can't express genuine feelings in effective ways. Many have lost the ability to recognize their emotions. Others repress feelings until they become so toxic that they burst through to the surface unexpectedly and explode in overwhelming and destructive ways. Those men who are aware of their emotions may try to numb them with alcohol and drugs, damaging their health in the process. Men need help in breaking through these barriers and in finding ways to express feelings in meaningful ways that enhance well-being and improve relationships.

Women who come for therapy, by contrast, often have their emotions so close to the surface that their feelings constantly get in the way of effective communication and negotiation in their daily lives and intimate relationships. They need help in keeping their emotions under control so that they can function effectively in the world. In our male-dominated society, it is difficult to get ahead when you're trembling or crying or showing uncertainty and fear.

The result of these gender differences in emotional health is that men's lack of emotional expression may end in lethal health problems, homicide, or suicide, while women's free emotional expression causes them to be more depressed and stressed throughout their longer lives. In *The Deadly Emotions,* Ernest Johnson states, "Anger, hostility, and aggression have recently emerged from the black box that contains our worst wishes and thoughts to be considered as potential risk factors for cardiovascular diseases and other health problems. . . . Anger, particularly when manifested as chronic hostility, has recently been linked with the Type A behavior pattern, coronary heart disease (CHD), death from CHD and malignant neoplasms, and death from all causes combined. Interestingly enough, a number of studies relate high levels of anger and hostility to the classic risk factors (e.g., cholesterol, smoking, drinking) that have been shown to predict heart disease, cancer, and other major health problems" (p. 7).

Gender differences in emotional expression appear early in life. There is recent evidence that little boys may be more subject to depression than are little girls, and it is no wonder when we look at how little boys are forced to deny their true feelings in order to act like men.

By the time these boys become men they have learned to subvert their emotions through stoicism, intellectualism, belligerence, or substance abuse.

"If I could teach just one more class," said eighty-eight-year-old Brian, a few months before his death, "I would teach men how to cry." Brian was a retired college professor who had spent most of his adult years living in his head. He was a theologian and a philosopher. He spent his days writing his observations of others at the retirement village where he lived and he kept up an active correspondence with a wide variety of other intellectuals from all parts of the world. When he wasn't writing, he spent time with his wife, who was very ill, in the nursing home adjacent to his apartment building.

Brian was skilled at articulating intellectualizations about his own aging and his wife's illness. He was also skilled at avoiding discussion about the emotional impact of these things on his life. Then he suffered a stroke at age eighty-seven. Until that time, whenever anyone asked a question that touched on his emotions, he would quickly think of an example from literature or another person's life to dodge his own emotional experiences.

After Brian's stroke, he was not able to control the emotions that seemed to surge up from deep inside. In the middle of a conversation, large sobs would begin to roll up from his midsection; he would gasp for breath and his eyes would fill with tears. I could watch these emotions bubble up while he looked at me helplessly because they were so unfamiliar to him.

As he was prone to do with other aspects of his life, Brian began to examine these emotional outbursts in a philosophical light and came to the conclusion that his sobs were a good thing and that men needed to learn how to cry at earlier ages. He spent his last months thinking about how he might go about teaching the ultimate course that would have been of benefit to him in preparing for the travails of old age. One of the last things that he said to me was that I should teach this course for him because he knew that he would not recover to help other men learn this important lesson, which he had discovered much too late.

Brian is an example of the many men I have had the privilege of working with as they approached death in very old age. These men have had wonderful, productive lives and have been caring, responsible professionals—but they have struggled to contain the emotions that eventually caught up with them as they lost more and more control of themselves and others. These men have always been in control of their emotions, just as they have controlled most other aspects of life. They can talk about emotions. They're tolerant of emotions in others. But they've always held themselves apart and sometimes even above others by denying their own need to express personal feelings. Yet when these men reach old age and become powerless in ill health, they are often like little children, overwhelmed by the unfamiliar emotions that have finally broken through all the years and years of masculine training that teach little boys and strong men not to cry.

Such repression of emotion has been shown to be linked to life-threatening disease. For example, Lydia Temoshok, a psychologist at the University of California at San Francisco, studied emotional expression among cancer patients. She found that those who did not feel comfortable in venting negative emotions such as sadness, depression, or fear when dealing with their disease had more aggressive tumor growth and more relapses than patients who were able to express their feelings more freely.

Unfortunately, our society encourages repression of emotion and discourages expressiveness. Over the past few decades, many women have enrolled in courses to learn how to control their emotions, to speak up when they feel hurt, and to respond in ways that men will understand. Women have been told that crying or throwing a temper tantrum is not a way to make it in a man's world, and they have been trying to comply in order to get ahead. The fear that women will be too emotional was brought home to me when I was confronted with unfair treatment in my own life.

A few years ago, I was denied tenure at the university where I worked as an administrator and a professor. I was the first woman to come up for tenure in that particular academic department in about twenty years. I had received good annual reviews for each of the five years leading to the time for a decision on my tenure, and I felt secure and confident. However, the all-male tenure committee decided that I had not met their criteria for tenure because I was one publication short of departmental standards. By my count, I had met the criteria but they refused to count several of my publications, especially a book chapter that had not yet been published. Needless to say, I was shocked—very angry and hurt.

I was emotional. I cried. I stormed. I yelled. I told everyone I knew about this injustice. I immediately began an appeal of the decision on procedural grounds and then, when I discovered that they had earlier tenured a male professor with the same publication record as mine, on the grounds of sex discrimination.

I had strong support from both men and women colleagues and friends—but their support and advice showed amazing gender differences. The men seemed almost embarrassed for me and felt that I should keep my situation quiet and pursue it through closed-door meetings according to university policy. My male friends gave me lots of advice about whom I should go to see and what procedural steps I needed to take. They wanted me to win my appeal and they admonished me not to "get emotional" and not to "take it personally."

My women colleagues had completely different reactions. They encouraged me to make it public and they helped me publicize my unfair treatment. They felt that I had been wronged and that the more people who knew about it, the safer I would be—and the more success I would have in fighting the injustice. They did not give me as much procedural advice but offered to go with me to take notes and to lend emotional support when I met with university officials and documented my accomplishments. They recognized that I was emotionally upset and needed someone along who would be thinking clearly and who could help me remember my questions and record the answers I received. They fully understood and supported my emotional upheaval and they knew that this was personally upsetting as well as professionally threatening. They not only understood my emotions, they shared in them and felt equally outraged.

I eventually won my fight and was awarded tenure. I am convinced that my women friends and my emotional expression were what got me through a very troubling period. I will always appreciate the support that my men friends gave me, but this experience afforded me first-hand experience with the differences men and women have in integrating emotions into other aspects of their lives. My emotions are very much a part of who I am. I value that and cannot and would not even want to ignore my emotional self as I go about the business of living.

Stress

Many people believe that men must die sooner because of environmental stressors and cultural expectations. For the people who believe this to be true, there is definitely a difference in how men and women respond. Men say, "Women live longer because men work harder than women. . . . Women have it easier than men." Charles is an example of a man with this attitude.

> "Women have it easier than men. I have to come to work every day to make the living, while my wife gets to do what she wants." Charles says this with tongue in cheek, but also with some conviction. Of course, Charles would be lost without his work and his breadwinner's role. His wife, Judy, also works, but she is a university professor and can schedule her own time so that she has much more flexibility. Even though she makes a good salary, her income is considered supplementary.
>
> After their four children were grown, Judy returned to school to earn her doctorate. She is just now getting started in a tenure-track faculty position, while Charles is beginning to think about retirement from his business. She is loving her new life at the same time he is feeling somewhat burned out after forty years in a very demanding profession.

By contrast, women who agree that stress and cultural expectations are the culprits tend to respond, "Men can't handle stress as well as women so they die earlier." Mary certainly feels this way about the death of her husband.

> "Men have to worry about so many things and they are not able to handle stress like women," says Mary, an eighty-six-year-old widow. "My husband was never able to get over the loss of our son [who died in the Vietnam War] . . . he kind of withdrew and just seemed to go downhill after that happened. I got through it by reminding myself that I was not the only mother who had lost a son and by telling myself that I must get on with my life. I made it a point to find out who the other boys were that died with my son and I contacted their mothers. We helped each other a lot and still keep in touch to this day."

Gender difference in coping and adapting to stress is an important issue that shows up in almost all dimensions of life. It has been the subject of much research. The ways in which men and women handle stress are demonstrated in such characteristics as seeking help when needed, juggling multiple roles, and being flexible and resilient when faced with obstacles, setbacks, and tragedy.

Emotion and Behavior

Throughout life, women are diagnosed with depression and anxiety in much greater numbers than are men. Men are diagnosed with more behavioral and substance abuse disorders. In other words, women feel bad and men act out. These emotional disorders result from trauma or dissatisfaction with life and from biochemical processes within the brain and nervous system. It is usually not clear which comes first, the dissatisfaction or the brain chemistry. In any event, the biochemical processes are treated with medication and the trauma and dissatisfactions are treated with psychotherapy. Women get more of both kinds of treatment, medication and psychotherapy, than do men.

Women's depression seems to peak during midlife and then slowly decline with advanced age, so that women, as a whole, are less depressed in old age than they were when they were younger. Men report lower levels of depression in early life but have steady increases as they age, so that by the time they reach old age their levels of reported depression are approximately equal to those of women. It seems that women are either increasingly satisfied with life or learn to cope with their emotions better as they grow older so that they start feeling better, whereas men become more dissatisfied and start feeling worse. Depression and despair can be deadly at any age, but seem especially difficult for older men who have not experienced such emotions at earlier times in their lives.

SUICIDAL BEHAVIOR White men over sixty-five years of age present the highest suicide risk in our society. They have had more power, money, and privilege than women and ethnic minorities throughout life, yet they seem to be the least prepared to cope with the issues of growing old. Many of these men visited their physicians only a few days before their suicides, yet their doctors (also primarily white men) did not pick up on the indicators that these patients were in such emotional distress that they wanted to kill themselves. These same doctors, however, diagnose women as depressed and prescribe antidepressant medication in record quantities for them. Among the clients and research participants I have known, much of the older men's emotional distress is going unrecognized and the older women's emotional expressiveness is being overmedicated by their physicians.

Of course, women also commit suicide. They actually attempt suicide more often than men, but they generally choose less lethal means. Men tend to use guns, car accidents, and hanging, all of which allow little leeway for rescue or second thoughts. Women tend to use an overdose of pills, where there is a chance that someone will discover them before death occurs. This leaves the opportunity to intervene with treatment for the despair that women are feeling in their lives.

Because men tend to hide their despair and to use such lethal means for taking their own lives, it is crucial that health professionals learn to recognize suicide indicators early and take them seriously.

"I have nothing to live for," said Frank, a seventy-eight-year-old man whose daughter had brought him in for counseling. "Since my wife died a year ago, I don't enjoy anything and I can't talk to anybody because they just don't understand how it is. . . . Last week I went over to my daughter's house for Thanksgiving dinner. My kids and grand-kids were there but I was so lonely because this is the first Thanksgiving since my wife died. They didn't seem to take much notice and finally, I just left and went out for a walk by myself because I was hurting so much."

Frank's daughter was surprised to learn that her dad was feeling lonely and hurt. His behavior that day had led the family to believe that he was angry and wanted to be left alone. He had seemed irritated by the children and restless throughout dinner. When he got up to leave, he said nothing but just stormed out the door as though he was mad about something. The family was confused about what to do about their father.

Frank had always appeared to be the dominant partner in the marriage and everyone believed that his wife was the more dependent one. But, now, with her death, Frank's dependence on his wife for meaning in life, for socialization, for relationships with their children, was emerging. She was the one who could interpret what he was feeling and could communicate that to the children. Without her, family communication was not working. His children were worried about him but couldn't get him to talk to them about what was troubling him. They realized that they didn't really know much about his emotional state and didn't know how to interpret what he was feeling when he refused to talk to them. They loved him but were at a loss about what he wanted or how to help him.

The fact was that he didn't know how to talk to anyone except his wife about his worries, his fears, his despair. Now she was gone and he was alone with no emotional support or resources to sustain him. He was thinking about suicide. He was planning to have a car accident, so no one would suspect that he had planned his own death. "I could run into a tree at a high speed," he said. "That way I would be out of my misery and everyone will think that I had a heart attack or a stroke or something that caused the accident."

Frank is an example of many of the older men I have seen for therapy in later life. These men are lost without their wives. The loss of a spouse can cut men off from a powerful source of their identity and leave them feeling overwhelming despair about who they are and what meaning they will ever have in life again. If the death or incapacity of the wife is coupled with personal health problems, some men are thrown into a crisis state that puts them at risk of suicide.

HOMICIDAL BEHAVIOR Anger and despair that builds up in men at all ages can result in homicide as well as suicide. Multiple murders of innocent people in a home, an office, a school, or some other public place are not uncommon in this country. Almost without exception these killers are men, many of whom are angry, depressed, and suicidal, and who have reached a crisis point in their lives that gets acted out in violence. Little is known about these men because they so often take their own lives along with those of their victims, leaving the so-called experts to make hypotheses about what may have been in the men's minds.

Luckily, many people with repressed hostility are brought to therapy before taking violent action and receive treatment so that such tragedies are avoided. After many years as a psychotherapist, I continue to be surprised and amazed at the levels of violent thoughts and feelings that some men reveal in therapy.

Sam sat at the window of the retirement home, looking out at people passing by, and thinking of how many he could wipe out with the gun he used to keep with him when he was working on the ranch. He was a tall, lean, tough man of the outdoors. His work life had been very demanding and he had prided himself on being able to outwork men only half his age. Now, at seventy-six, his wife was dead and his five children had decided that he would be better off living in this godforsaken place for old people. He didn't know where else to go because he needed someone to cook and clean for him. His children obviously didn't want him to live with them and the doctor said that he needed supportive nursing care for his health problems.

He had no interest in getting to know the other people in his new home. He was mad and obsessed with thoughts of getting even with someone, anyone, for the way he was ending up. He just wished that he had some way of getting his gun so that he could either kill himself or kill someone else as retribution for his troubles.

And the elderly aren't alone in their anger. In almost every town and city in our country, we hear of street violence and drive-by shootings by gangs of adolescents or young adults. As I discussed earlier, the overwhelming majority of these perpetrators are young men—and so are the majority of their victims. In the earlier part of this century, the lives of young men were sacrificed in foreign countries during war. Today, it seems that the wars are in our streets but with the same result, the sacrifice of young men and boys. Male violence is robbing many men and some women of the chance to grow old.

LOVE AND COMBAT Feelings of closeness, affection, and intimacy are also difficult for many men to express. Men learn how to be intimate through sex. Women develop a greater repertoire of intimate expression than do men. Women complain that with any sign of affection men immediately want to engage in sex. Men complain that women are too sentimental or that they tease about sex rather than being honest about what they want. Women want attention and expansion of the loving feelings. Men want action and release of emotion.

> Tom, as a divorced man of forty, became nervous about commitment and backed off from any woman who began to send him cards, notes, or leave telephone messages of affection on his answering machine. These things signified much too much closeness for him and he lost interest in such women very quickly. Of course, he always began to have sex with these women as soon as they would consent, usually very early in their relationship. He felt that sex only meant that he enjoyed being with them in the moment. Sex was his way of feeling close without commitment. For the women, sex was the beginning of a loving relationship and they began to express that closeness in a variety of other ways, without realizing that they were writing the death notice on their time with Tom.
>
> Tom used alcohol and cigarettes as a means of self-medicating his loneliness and his need for intimacy. When he was sober, he described feelings of inadequacy and needing to prove himself as a man in order to be okay in the eyes of others and of himself. When he was drunk, he had fantasies of hand-to-hand combat with other men where he would be victorious for the good of some righteous cause. Though he had opposed the Vietnam War and had dodged the draft, he now felt he had wimped out and that he should have gone to fight so that he could have proven his masculinity.

He developed a tremor in his hands and sometimes in his voice when he spoke of his rage and his fear of affection and intimacy. He often harbored suicidal and homicidal thoughts against himself and other males. Though he was functioning adequately in his everyday life and had the reputation of being a sensitive ladies' man, Tom was in danger of doing harm to himself or others if he didn't find a way to come to terms with his own sense of masculinity and isolation.

The need to do combat in order to prove masculinity is something that I have seen often with men in their middle years. These men, who think they haven't proven themselves in some macho way, feel unworthy of love and shamed by feelings of cowardice. Many times they cannot be intimate with others for fear that their secret will be found out. They are distant from their children and may project their feelings onto sons, living vicariously and prodding their boys to be the man that they never were.

I suspect that much of the violence that we are now experiencing in our society is an aftermath of the Vietnam War. The young men who went to that war more than a generation ago were exposed to circumstances that have left them with lifetime emotional scars. The young men of today are sons of the Vietnam experiences and are living out their fathers' legacies of horror, shame, and desensitization. And so the killing goes on in our streets rather than on some foreign soil, and the deaths of these young men continue to be included in the statistics that show men to have lower life expectancies than women.

JOY AND AFFECTION Just as the negative expression of sadness, depression, and anger is squelched for men in our society, so is the positive expression of joy and love. It is interesting to watch a man and a woman with a little baby. The woman is more apt to act silly, to talk baby talk, to kiss and hug this lovable little creature. The same is true with the outward expression of love for pets.

I love to see men show their love and emotional attachment to children, to act silly with them, and to be soft and gentle in ways that children really respond to. But most men let women take this role, while they stoically put up the Christmas lights on the outside of the house or sign their name to the birthday greetings and have no idea what the gift inside the package is because they were not involved in the purchase. Expressing love, joy, and affection are too often the job of women. Men are missing out because these are the things that bind us together and give meaning to our lives when all else, like jobs and power, is gone.

Men who make it to old age sometimes become more affectionate, but it may be at a great price, as in the situation of Roy.

Roy was suffering from Alzheimer's disease and family members were in conflict about what to do about his care. As they met to discuss their options, Roy's children and grandchildren described their relationship with him. It became apparent that he was not a person who had shown much love and affection for his children. He was a workaholic, a strict disciplinarian, and a man who believed in the old adages, "spare the rod and spoil the child" and "idle hands are the devil's playground."

His sons were bitter because their father had never attended their ball games or been there for them when they needed him. They felt close to their mother and wanted to protect her from the burden of caregiving for their father. They felt strongly that their father should be placed in a nursing home.

The daughters were not so sure about this. They agreed that their dad hadn't been loving and affectionate, but he had been less strict with them and they felt an obligation to care for him at home. Since his illness, his behavior had changed dramatically and he had begun to show affection to his wife and daughters. He would give them hugs, show appreciation for their care, and tell them that he loved them. As his brain became more disordered, he was becoming more like the loving father that they had always hoped for. They were reluctant to give that up even if it meant personal sacrifice in caring for him.

The grandchildren in this family had known Roy as a different man from the one his children described. While he was not overly affectionate, they remembered that he had shown interest in their activities once he had retired. He had helped them with projects and had enlisted them to help him plant his flower and vegetable gardens. They were surprised that their own fathers felt so negative about him. They also felt that he should be kept at home with the whole family pitching in to help with his care. The family was deadlocked about what to do. Eventually, because the women were willing to provide the care, the men reluctantly agreed to help out when they could.

Roy and Brian never learned how to express emotions. It was not until the travails of old age and disease took their toll that they were able at last to let others know how they felt deep inside. How different their lives might have been if they had only been able to cry when they were hurting and to show affection when they felt love.

INTELLECTUAL DEVELOPMENT

Mental health is not only based on emotions but also on the abilities to think, learn, remember, solve problems, and make judgments. While men and women have very few differences in overall general intelligence, they often take different approaches to understanding problems, to making judgments, and to engaging in intellectual activities. Both men and women seem to have the same brainpower—but they learn to apply it differently. Perhaps one reason why women live longer than men is that they become better skilled at solving the little problems in life that are important to longevity.

There is an old joke about the wife who says, "My husband makes all the important decisions in our marriage. I only decide about little things like where we'll live, how to raise the children, and how to pay our bills. He has to worry about the big issues like world peace, the global economy, and protection of the environment."

Women gain experience in solving problems like how to manage a household, how to get support from others when they need it, how to interact with a wide variety of people, and how to live in reasonable comfort on a tight budget. Men—having sweated the big issues and left the little things up to a woman as long as there was one available—often find themselves in old age without adequate skills to function on their own or to communicate with others in satisfying ways. Although the intellectual pursuits that motivated men in earlier times remain important to their satisfaction and well-being in late life, men often fail to thrive for lack of the ability to apply practical knowledge and skills to everyday problems of living.

Formal and Informal Education

Education has been shown to be linked to longer lives and greater life satisfaction. Many of the men I know who have reached the age of eighty-five or older have been lifelong scholars. They read. They study. They love to debate ideas and engage in intellectual discourse. These men have often completed college degrees in engineering, ministry, education, or liberal arts. Some have been self-educated after high school and have been involved in a variety of occupations. Many were probably considered nerds in their younger years. Clearly, they were not macho men or sports jocks. They valued learning and continue to engage in their individual intellectual pursuits. These men also either have a wife or they live in a retirement community where the necessities of life—meals, housekeeping, social activities—are provided for them by professional staff, so they don't have to worry about basic survival tasks.

Women, too, engage in intellectual pursuits throughout life but in different ways from older men. Most of the older women of today have not been fortunate enough to get college educations. The few older women who did were often teachers. For example, last year I was asked to speak at a sixtieth class reunion for the university where I teach. I expected the group would consist mostly of men and their wives, but I was wrong. The fifteen or twenty people who attended this reunion were almost all women who had obtained their teaching degrees six decades earlier and had spent many years working in education. Some of them had never married and others had married late because in their day they were not allowed to be married and continue teaching. They had to choose between marriage and career.

Because of this, a college degree was considered a waste of time and money for a woman. And some women of past generations were denied higher education, so they learned practical skills and educated themselves in informal ways as that was their only recourse. As a result, they are masters in seeking out learning experiences that can be applied to everyday living.

For both men and women in late life, intellectual pursuits provide distraction from physical disabilities and pain and can be an important motivation for living in spite of health problems. Elsie is such a person.

> Elsie, a ninety-year-old woman, is almost blind and has very painful angina due to heart problems. She has been so depressed that the staff at the retirement center where she lives asked me to visit with her and make recommendations about how they could help her. On my first interview with this frail woman, I realized that her health problems and her pain were only part of the reason she was in so much despair. During our second meeting, she revealed her hopelessness regarding her inability to read, write, and play the piano. The loss of these important activities in her life was troubling her much more than the angina.
>
> As a girl, she had been an excellent student and was musically talented. When she graduated from high school, her father decided that

it wasn't worth the money for his daughter to go to college—she would marry and wouldn't need further education to take care of a husband and children. Her brothers both attended college but she had to stay at home and teach piano lessons to the children in the neighborhood.

In spite of this setback, Elsie had continued to educate herself, reading everything she could get her hands on. She also wrote short stories for her own satisfaction but had never tried to publish her work. By age twenty, she was married and lived a traditional life of wife and mother, except that she never gave up her voracious appetite for knowledge. She saved money and advocated for her own daughters to go to college. She was very proud that all four of her children had college degrees. She was especially happy that one daughter had gone on to graduate school and received a Ph.D. Her children now lived in distant states and were not around to visit her very often. This hadn't bothered Elsie because she was content to be with her books, papers, and piano, but now she had neither intellectual stimulation nor family support.

For a person like Elsie, vision impairment is perhaps the worst thing that can happen. Without sight, she no longer wanted to live. She couldn't imagine life without her books and the type of intellectual activity that had given meaning to her for so long. She could tolerate the physical pain, but she couldn't accept the boredom. Consulting with her physician, I was able to initiate a change in medication that helped her angina pain. I worked with the staff to arrange for a tape player and books on tape for her to listen to. One of my graduate students began to visit with her each week. All these things helped to relieve Elsie's depression, but she had to accept her dependence on others in a way she had never experienced before.

With women's movement toward greater equality, the pursuit of intellectual goals is much more possible now than ever before in history. Women of all ages are taking advantage of these changes. After centuries of being denied equal opportunity for development, women are now enrolling in both formal and informal education in record numbers. Women, who in earlier times were forced to drop out of high school or were denied entrance into universities, now outnumber men in completion of the Graduate Equivalency Degree (GED) and in college admissions. With increased educational opportunities, the lives and intellectual health of tomorrow's older women should be enhanced. Their job opportunities will be greatly improved as well, so that the coming generations of elder women should have better economic resources and life satisfaction in old age than the current one does.

DIFFERENCES IN LATE-LIFE LEARNING

Many of the women and men who survive into very old age keep mentally healthy by engaging in new learning experiences. Women tend to seek out organized classes and educational tours and trips with others, where there is a guide or a facilitator and other learners to be connected with. If there is no class or group available, women will often organize their own discussion or support group. Women like the socialization of learning. They enroll, bring their friends, and make new friends. Sylvia is a very positive role model for lifelong learning.

Sylvia is an eighty-year-old artist. She had taken some art courses in high school and college, but had little time to do art while she was rearing her seven children. After her kids were grown and her husband had died, she began taking art courses at the university. One of her professors arranged an exhibit of her work. This was like starting a whole new life—not only was she doing something that she loved, she was gaining recognition as a serious artist for the first time.

Sylvia was encouraged to begin producing more artwork, but soon found that spending time alone all day in her studio was isolating. She felt disconnected from others, so she organized a local art group where others like her could meet to learn and to critique each other's work. This grew into plans for an annual show for their group. Now the initiative of this one elder woman has resulted in a cultural event for the entire community that expands every year.

Older men tend to pursue learning activities on their own, where they can be in charge, rather than take instruction or guidance from others. Many older men are solitary learners like Zach.

Eighty-five-year-old Zach loves the Internet. In his earlier days, he was a ham radio operator; now he has taught himself all about computers. I met him through his grandson, Rich, who was in my class. Rich said, "You ought to interview my granddad for your book. He is one of the most interesting people I know."

Zach has many health problems and can hardly get around anymore because of a bad hip. He relies on his wife for day-to-day companionship and he's close to his family. Because of his health problems, he's not able to get out and about as he once did. Instead, he travels in cyberspace on his computer throughout much of the day while his wife is gone from home, getting her exercise and doing church work. He was in obvious pain as we sat talking but he managed to maintain a wry sense of humor and to tease his wife every chance he got during our conversation. It was apparent that the computer is integral to his life now and that his ability to learn and pursue this interest keeps him involved and connected to the world. In addition, he feels empowered because he knows more about the Internet than the younger members of his family. As I left, we exchanged e-mail addresses; the next morning when I returned to my office there was a message on my computer from my new cyberspace friend.

Older men also thrive on mentoring and teaching others. One of my mentors in my doctoral studies was a very formal man who was called Mr. K by everyone who knew him. He felt duty bound to teach others for as long as he lived.

Mr. K had been a university professor and, until his death at age ninety-six, was still mentoring college students. He was a designated foster grandparent to one of the sororities at the nearby university and he participated in every class and research project that was conducted at the retirement center where he lived. His motto for living was "use it or lose it" and he subscribed to the belief that everyone should foster "constructive discontent." By staying discontented, he believed that he kept his mind sharp and active.

He would write long letters to the administrator about ways in which the retirement center could be run more efficiently. One letter was a recommendation that they change the square dining room tables to round ones. He had measured the space and calculated how many people could sit at each table and had determined that more people could be seated comfortably at round tables than at the current square tables. Another time he did a study of the use of the vending machines in the lobby and argued that these machines were used so seldom and were so unattractive that they should be taken out of the facility. He also felt compassion for the community cat, who was being made crazy by having so many people claim ownership. He kept behavioral records on the cat to gather evidence that it would be better off with a family rather than living in the retirement center.

Mr. K kept his strength up by working out daily on an exercise bike, but this was a boring activity for him so he made it more

productive by watching the numbers change on the odometer and fig-
uring their square roots and factors. He stayed connected to distant
family members by debating about books and politics in letters. One
of his granddaughters was getting a doctorate in philosophy and he
especially loved to share ideas and to read the same books as she. They
would start a book together and send it back and forth through the
mail with sections underlined and highlighted for the other.

Mr. K believed that he had a lifelong responsibility to teach younger
people. Unfortunately, most younger people and the staff did not recognize the rich resource that this frail, very old man could be to their
own learning and many did not appreciate his attempts to teach them
ways to do things better.

I discovered him when I was recruiting people to participate in a
life review group. I was attracted to him immediately and he loved the
respect and attention that I gave him for his wealth of knowledge and
wisdom. He was extremely pleased to be listed in the acknowledgments
section of my dissertation, where I gave credit to all the people who
had been instrumental in my education. As a graduation gift, he gave
me his pin from an honorary society for outstanding scholarship to
which he had belonged as a young professor. I took this as a great compliment and symbol of his respect for my intellectual development
during the time I had known him. After I graduated and became a
professor myself, our intellectual relationship continued until his
death, first by written correspondence, then by exchange of taped mes-
sages when he could no longer write.

For men like Mr. K and Brian, who have not been able to freely
express their emotions, the connections that teaching and intellectual
mentoring bring are very important to their well-being. Their intellectual health stayed strong in spite of the fact that their physical health
was very poor.

One successful program that I've initiated for my gerontology students is called "Partners in the Classroom." I invite elders to join me
in teaching graduate level classes about the issues of aging. The classes
meet at the retirement center once a month and my coteachers, who
are usually in their eighties and nineties, talk with the students about
issues like family concerns, health problems, and attitudes on sex,
death, and dying. This program is life changing for the students and
life enhancing for the elders. The students find that, contrary to popular belief, older people can be mentally sharp and intellectually

sophisticated. The elders feel empowered as teachers and authorities and they interact with each other in ways that are not usual in their everyday lives. This is one group activity where men participate in equal numbers to women. In fact, the women often have to be encouraged because they don't think of themselves as university teachers and worry that they'll have little to offer graduate students.

One man who helped initiate this program suffered a stroke and became widowed within the same year. Later he returned to help out with the class even though he had trouble remembering words and expressing himself adequately. During the course of the latest class, he had another stroke and was hospitalized. When some students went to visit him, he was overjoyed and promised them that he would be back in class as soon as he could. He felt motivated and responsible to these students because of the intellectual connection that the program provided.

MENTAL HEALTH AND LONGEVITY

Emotional and intellectual well-being are strongly linked to physical health and longevity. Anger, fear, hostility, depression, and aggression all take their toll on our arteries, organs, and desire to live. Love, laughter, affection, and joy keep us connected to others and give us reasons to get up each morning and face a new day. Men and women who have survived into old age somehow find a balance between emotional expressiveness and stress management skills to deal effectively with the problems that they inevitably encounter. Those who do not find such coping methods succumb to disease or despair.

As women develop better assertiveness skills and obtain more formal education, they're able to get better jobs and medical treatment. These two things alone will ensure them increased longevity and a higher quality of life. Men still have a long way to go in learning to vent their emotions in constructive, health-promoting ways and to reduce the destructive effects of anger, hostility, and aggression that threaten their chances of living into old age.

I've often heard it said that the brain is our most important sex organ. From what I've observed and studied about the powers of the mind, I would go even further and proclaim that the mind has such strong impact on all body functioning that mental health is integral to long life. The will and determination to live is vital to resiliency and survival. Our emotions and intellect cannot be ignored in the search for the secrets of longevity.

CHAPTER SIX

Social Health:
Our Relationships, Ourselves

———

W hen it comes to relationships, women are like smoke alarms and men are like shock absorbers. Women, like smoke alarms, are sensitive to the environment around them. They notice when something is not quite right and they try to get others to notice too, so that the problem can get evaluated and corrected as soon as possible. Shock-absorbing men fend off stress and strive to stay calm, logical, and objective. They want to keep things on a even keel as long as possible so that the stress is not disruptive or even noticeable.

Women appear to be more emotionally invested in relationships than men. Indeed, women are often criticized for codependence in relationships, an assertion that adds to their stress levels, their emotional problems, and even their safety concerns in cases where violence is a factor. Yet in the long run, most women develop reciprocal support systems that serve them well at those times in life when they need help from others.

Many years ago, Barbra Streisand had a hit song containing the line "People who need people are the luckiest people in the world." I used to find the words curious because, in our culture, people who need people are considered not lucky but dependent. We are taught that dependence is bad and independence is the road to maturity, respect, and success. We learn to be autonomous and to view people who need others as insufficient and even mentally ill. There is an entire industry built up around the stigma of codependence. Go to the self-help or pop psychology rack in any bookstore and you will find shelves full of books about codependence. Mental health centers and psychiatric hospitals market treatment programs for the condition and one of our greatest fears about getting old is that we will become dependent on others.

But since I've been studying longevity and interviewing people who have lived into very old age, I've come to understand dependence in a new light. I now believe that the words of the song are correct—people who really need people are more likely to put time and energy into seeking out and developing friendships and intimate relationships. They form relationships with others and build a network of people they can depend on for support when they need it. People with good social health have relationships that are interdependent and complementary, where each person helps the other, where each takes care of and is taken care of as necessary. Such interdependent relationships provide the safety net that is important for survival throughout life but is especially crucial in old age.

Women *are* luckier than men in this regard because women tend to build better social support systems and develop more reciprocity and interdependence in their friendships. In old age, when they need help, they are more familiar with dependence and are not so resistant to seeking help and relying on others for assistance. Men who have been forced to be strong, independent, and self-sufficient from the time they were little boys don't have the same skills to build adequate reciprocal relationships in their old age. Their masculine pride often prohibits them from seeking help when they need it. That makes them very unlucky at a time when they need luck the most.

COMPETITION AND COOPERATION

Boys are pushed to separate from others almost from the day they are born. They are held and cuddled less than girls. Parents play with them in a more rough-and-tumble manner. They are pushed to be separate from their mothers and from others.

"Don't be a Mama's boy!" "Be a man!" "Do it on your own." "Be the best." "Go for the glory." All these dictums encourage boys to compete with each other, which serves to isolate them by promoting individual accomplishment attained by outperforming everyone else. While these organized activities provide camaraderie among teammates, they also promote hierarchical relationships based on who wins and who loses.

Boys win by making others lose. They win by beating up on others. They earn praise for being on top and ridicule for losing and being on the bottom. Only the best is good enough and anything less is failure. This puts boys in the bind of always having to put someone else down to feel good about themselves.

Gaining power over someone else and being respected by proving your strength is often important for being accepted by other boys. Susan recalls her tomboy days and her initiation into the boys' group.

"I was the only boy in my neighborhood who was a girl," says twenty-five-year-old Susan, who describes herself as a tomboy. "I didn't like to play with the girls. I wanted to play ball and hang out with the boys. They accepted me only if I would act tough and get into fights with other boys." With tears in her eyes, she describes how she discovered a way to be respected and included by the boys. "I found one boy who was weaker than me and I beat him up every day. Everyone made fun of him because he couldn't hold his own with a girl. He was humiliated, but I was accepted as one of the guys. Now I feel rotten about the way I treated him and probably ruined his life so that I could get approval from the guys."

Susan's story is unusual for a girl, but is common for many boys. They learn to prey on someone weaker so that they will feel strong and be admired by their peers. As a young woman, Susan is now struggling to find connections that do not put her in the position of hurting others so she can succeed. She realizes that her hurtful actions to others alienated her from herself and left her feeling angry and empty. She may have gained approval from the boys but now she doesn't approve of herself.

Girls are not pushed like boys to compete with others. Tomboys like Susan are atypical and people assume that they will grow out of their aggressiveness. Girls are encouraged, even expected, to nurture relationships with others, especially their families. They do not have to separate from their mothers to learn how to be an adult woman. Girls are programmed to share their toys, clothes, food, and lives with others. They are rewarded for cooperation rather than for competitive accomplishments.

Most women report that they work best in a collaborative rather than a competitive situation. They express their competitiveness by competing with themselves toward individual achievement rather than against other people where someone would have to end up losing so that one person can win. Striving to be the best that one can be is very beneficial in successful aging and surviving the problems that are encountered with illness and loss. Competing with others becomes less and less adaptive with age and can leave a person without the friends or social support system necessary for survival.

POWER AND SENSITIVITY

In our society, where males have the power and privilege as well as greater physical brawn, girls have to learn strategies for getting what they want through connecting with others and anticipating their desires and needs. They use cooperation and negotiation rather than competition for building relationships. Because women lack power and physical strength, they become more skilled than men at forming their relationships through cooperation rather than competition.

A woman develops sensitivities (often called intuition) to the moods and desires of others so that she can stay out of harm's way and maintain control of her environment. She learns to take the perspective of others, to understand how others might feel, so that she can better understand a situation before acting. Most men don't develop these subtle skills because they have the benefit of male privilege and physical brawn to get what they want. Those who are not physically strong or do not enjoy much power in their lives suffer terribly because they are held to the masculine standard of competitiveness, which results in much pressure and performance anxiety for the losers in a male hierarchical system. Some of these men become loners or batterers of women and children as they struggle with their feelings of inadequacy and incompetence.

The masculine model of competition results in men tending to act before they have thoroughly considered the thoughts and feelings of other people. They focus on the problem to be solved and take immediate action to find a resolution. Men expect that if their decision is just and good, then others will accept and support it. The feminine model for cooperation results in women tending to be reluctant to

take independent action. They want to understand how others feel
and how any actions will affect others who might be involved. They
want consensus about the resolution of a problem and are hesitant to
act on a solution until all the consequences for the individuals
involved have been thoroughly explored and agreed on.

Empathy and Problem Solving

I witness these differences over and over with graduate students learning to become counselors. Beginning counselors must develop
empathic rapport with their clients as well as the ability to analyze
their problems. These two things are difficult to do at the same time
because empathy requires relationship-building skills, while analysis
requires diagnostic and problem-solving skills. The empathic counselor must connect with clients and take their perspectives to understand their thinking, feeling, and behavior patterns. In other words,
counselors must be able to put themselves in the clients' shoes and see
the world through their eyes. At the same time, to help clients find
solutions to their problems, the counselor must be able to stand apart
from the clients' perspectives, to analyze what is actually going on, and
to devise methods of resolving their problems. Therefore, a skilled
counselor balances his or her abilities to connect with and understand
the client's feelings with abilities to stand apart from and analyze the
client's problems.

More often than not, it is the women students who have highly
developed empathic skills. They come to the counseling situation with
abilities for establishing rapport, making connections, exploring feelings, and understanding the other person's point of view. The male
students are more apt to focus on identifying the client's problem and
taking action to solve that problem. Of course, most men (especially
those who want to become counselors) have some empathy and most
women are also problem solvers, but I definitely notice a gender difference in the way students approach the counseling relationship and
how they feel most at ease and sure of their abilities.

In old age, there are no easy answers to many problems. The ability
to solve problems is important for older people—but it's crucial that
the older individual take time to consider all the options and understand what's in the best interests of everyone involved so as to live in
community with others. As people lose independence due to illness
or other problems, they must listen to others and be able to view

things from the perspective of other people if they are to get the help and cooperation they need.

MARRIAGE

Similar differences in attitude between empathy and problem solving are often behind the marital problems I see in people who come to me for therapy. Women want to talk about feelings and connect emotionally with their husbands or boyfriends, while men want to take action to resolve "the problem" without talking about feelings or processing what they regard as irrelevant things.

Men and women also frequently differ in their approaches to child rearing. Mothers want to talk to the kids to understand their behaviors and to help them understand the consequences. Fathers want to straighten out the behavior first—and when that is accomplished, they feel there is no real need to talk about anything unless the problem recurs.

Men and women also differ in their approaches to sex. Women like to talk first so as to feel close before engaging in sex. Men like to have sex first and then after sex they may feel close enough to risk the intimacy of talking. As a result, women look for people outside their marriages to talk to and men—if they talk to anybody about their fears, insecurities, and frustrations—usually talk only to their wives and no one else.

In studies that ask about the individuals in whom people confide, women will typically name several women friends and often do not list their husbands at all. A man tends to name fewer people and often only his wife. Studies like these confirm that women have greater options for supportive relationships whether or not they are close to their husbands. The lack of confidants for men leaves them vulnerable to isolation when they need help, especially if their wives die, become ill, or divorce them.

Oscar and Betty Lou illustrate the gender-based marital differences that leave men at risk in later life.

Oscar was worried about having enough money for retirement. He had worked hard all his life, often at two jobs requiring heavy manual labor, just to make ends meet. Now, at age sixty, with four kids grown and out on their own, he was bound and determined that he was going to save as much as possible for his retirement. The only problem was that he did not trust anyone with his money, not the banks, not any retirement funds, and not his wife, Betty Lou. He had waited too long to have this money for himself and he was not about to let anyone else have control of it.

Betty Lou had always stayed at home. She had been the primary caregiver for the children and was now caring for her ailing mother. She had never worked outside the home but had always managed the household budget and had been instrumental in scraping enough together to see that all their children got decent educations, which she and Oscar never had. She had no idea that her husband was hiding away money that he was earning by working overtime.

Then their son had an emergency. He needed $700 to pay an emergency hospital bill. He called his parents to see if they could help out. Betty Lou knew that they didn't have that kind of money in their savings account and was shocked when Oscar revealed that he had the money and told their son not to worry about it. Oscar felt good about helping his son, but Betty Lou felt betrayed and very angry to learn that her husband had been hiding money from her.

Oscar had never been much of a talker. Betty Lou had always had her mother, her children, and more recently her granddaughter to talk to, so although she complained about her husband's silent ways, she hadn't felt very lonely. Now she realized how little she and her husband had in common. This incident only served to bring a distressed relationship into harsh reality.

In counseling, this couple obviously still loved each other but had very different ways of viewing their relationship. Oscar felt isolated and had been that way for most of his life. He had been devoted to his wife and kids but was never around them much because he was always working. He didn't say much and couldn't understand why Betty Lou was so upset. He had always been faithful to her. He gave her his regular paycheck. He was only hiding his extra money and he planned to spend it for both of them to take trips together once he retired.

Betty Lou was finally releasing years of anger that she didn't even realize she had in her. She didn't doubt that Oscar would spend "his" money on her as he said, but she felt demeaned and discounted that he felt she would squander it. She was also upset that she had no say in the planning for "their" retirement. In the counseling sessions, they began to talk to each other genuinely for the first time in forty years of marriage.

Although Betty Lou had no money in her own right, she had options through the court to share in the assets that she and Oscar had accumulated over their years of marriage. She had good relationships with her children, grandchildren, and her sisters and brothers. Oscar, with his stash of money, was the person whose future was more at risk if they divorced—he would be truly alone without his wife. His children and grandchildren barely knew him because he had always been working and had hardly ever carried on a meaningful conversation with them in their whole lives. He had left that up to their mother. When it was pointed out to him how much he was risking by stubbornly refusing to include his wife in his plans for their future, he reluctantly arranged to put his savings in a joint account and to continue in counseling to see if they could learn to communicate and work out their differences.

This couple is an extreme example of what happens in many marriages; the wife's role is to keep the family connected while the husband's role is to keep the family financed. In times of marital conflict, the woman typically has more emotional support from friends and family members while the man has no one but the impersonal legal system and impartial courts to turn to for resolution of financial concerns.

Marital Separation

Another marriage was not salvageable. Although Don and Evelyn didn't divorce, it was too late for counseling to resolve the years of domination and lack of affection.

Seventy-year-old Evelyn's marriage to Don had never really been very satisfying for her. He always left her at home to care for the children while he pursued a high-powered, high-paying career. He would often go off on extended business trips and made no secret of having numerous affairs with other women. He had even fathered a child by one of the women in his office and supported this "second family" for many years. Evelyn longed for freedom from this insensitive man but they were Catholic and she didn't believe in divorce, plus she didn't know how she could manage on her own with three children. After the children were grown, she and her husband continued to live their separate lives. She belonged to several clubs, was active in the church, spent time with her many friends, and enjoyed working with her favorite charities. She had close relationships with her children, especially one daughter who lived close by. Her marriage was bad but overall her life was good. Then Don got sick.

As his health failed, he became severely depressed. Evelyn had to take over management of their money and she discovered that she had skills she had never known before. As she realized her capabilities, she became extremely angry about all the years she had wasted, all the years that Don had led her to believe that she was incapable of handling financial matters. Don, in his incapacitated state, also realized new things about himself. Now that he could no longer exert his power or his sexual prowess, he discovered that he loved his wife in ways that he had never felt before. He felt a deep appreciation for her care and he longed for closeness.

Evelyn would have no part of it. She was angry and felt trapped having to care for a husband that she had long since lost affection for. His need for care caused her to miss out on being with her friends and participating in other meaningful activities. She too became depressed and had to be hospitalized.

In counseling, this couple found no way to resolve their long-standing differences. With divorce out of the question, Evelyn moved out of the house into an apartment where she could have her own life. The children hired a caregiver for their father and he was left abandoned and alone as he had once abandoned his wife and family. Evelyn's depression lifted. She resumed her life with her friends and secretly felt that the turnabout was retribution for the abuse she had suffered in all the years of marriage to a man who took her for granted.

The damage that had been done to this relationship in earlier years was too severe for repair in late life. This husband later died in a nursing home with no one to care about him just as he had failed to care about his wife or family when he was younger, dominant, and in good health.

Widowhood

Of course, most late-life marriages aren't so dysfunctional as those I've just described. Most couples who stay together find ways to adapt to their differences that are mutually satisfying to both parties. Eventually, though, one person will be left alone when the other dies.

While widowhood is sad and lonely for both men and women who have had satisfying marriages, men fare worse than women in adjusting to being alone. Since men rely primarily on wives for companionship, confidences, and caretaking, they are not very well connected to others if they lose their wives. Women, who tend to have close friends and strong connections to family, don't rely so heavily on husbands for these basic needs and therefore don't feel so alone after the death of a husband. In fact, some women report a new sense of freedom after they get accustomed to being on their own, perhaps for the first time in their lives.

Often women have been providing caregiving for their husbands for extended periods before death. This can leave a woman feeling exhausted and isolated from her former connections. After the death of her spouse, she may be able to get back into the activities and relationships that gave meaning and enjoyment to her life before her husband's illness.

Seventy-five-year-old Carla began feeling very anxious and scared after her husband Jack died. He had suffered the long progressive deterioration of Alzheimer's disease, through which she had cared for him in their home until the last two weeks before his death. When he was first diagnosed, their relationship became closer as they faced the tragedy of his illness together and as a result of their constant companionship after he could no longer work. But after several years, his mind had slipped away and he was totally dependent on her for his every need. His personality changed so that he was no longer the person she had loved over the years. At times, he was combative and she had to call her daughter to come and help her control him. Through it all, though, she was glad that he could stay at home and that she had the health and strength to care for him. Then he died and she didn't know what to do with herself.

Before Jack's illness, Carla had been an outgoing, very social person. She entertained family and friends in her home and she loved to plan big, festive family gatherings during the holidays. It had been years now since she had been able to do that. Her friends had quit calling her to go places because they knew that she couldn't get away from her caregiving duties. When the children came home to visit, they spent most of their time taking care of home repairs, cleaning, and all the things around the house that she couldn't manage. There was no time or spirit for festivities. She had devoted herself to Jack's care and had let her own interests slide away.

In the last few weeks of Jack's life, he had to be hospitalized, and then, when he came home, Carla found that she was too exhausted to provide the added level of care that he needed. She had to hire help to care for her husband. He died two weeks later and she blamed herself because she wasn't strong enough to keep caring for him. She started having anxiety attacks and was referred by her physician for counseling.

After a few sessions of talking through all the feelings around her husband's death, her frustrations with his caregiving, her grief over the loss of her friends and former activities, and her relief that Jack finally knew some peace, Carla was able to start making some plans for herself. She planned some trips to visit her children. Then she reconnected with her old friends. She helped her minister start a support group for caregivers in her church. Her life became full and meaningful again, and she felt a new freedom that she had never known as a younger wife or as an older caregiver. Her anxiety decreased and her self-confidence soared to new heights.

On the surface, it may look as though men do better after the death of a spouse—they typically do not stay alone very long but remarry within months or a few years. However, this rush to remarry often indicates that men are much more dependent than women. Of course, there are also many more women available for older men to marry than there are men available to older women. I know many women who would like to be married again, if there were men available, but they make the best of their single life by surrounding themselves with family and friends. I also know many widows who would never consider remarriage because they don't want the restriction on their activities that marriage imposed and they fear they might end up having to provide care for yet another ailing husband.

FRIENDSHIP

Men will often name many more people as friends than women do. In a study that I did several years ago in a retirement center, the men would claim that all the members of the staff were their friends, as well as numerous other people with whom they came in casual contact. The women I interviewed rarely named the staff as their friends. They tended to define friendship as relationships that had depth and meaning in their lives.

Men often think of acquaintances or coworkers as friends. While women might feel friendly with such people, however, they reserve the title of *friend* for a few special relationships in their lives. Women will often name family members (such as sisters or daughters) as friends because they are their closest confidantes and are the people whom they turn to first in times of trouble. These gender differences in friendship take on increased importance in times of illness or financial difficulty.

Forty-year-old Mel was severely depressed and so was his wife, Freda. He had been a fairly successful salesman and had felt contented with his family life, or so he thought. But in the past few months, his company had merged with another and his new boss was putting the pressure on for more sales and increased sales contacts. He wasn't happy at work and was afraid that he might lose his job if he didn't measure up to these new standards. His wife had recently taken a part-time job since the kids were all in school. As a result she was more stressed and less available to him than she used to be.

Mel began to have thoughts of suicide and felt that his wife and children could get along fine without him. Freda also felt depressed and worried about Mel, so she came in for counseling. It soon became apparent that it was Mel who was in need of therapy more than Freda. As he talked about his stress and his resources for support, he revealed that he had no close friends. When asked to list his friends, he could only think of his customers and one high school friend that he hadn't seen or talked to in twenty years. This was a complete shock to him because he had always felt that he had good friends. But when he needed a real friend, there was no one for him to turn to but his wife.

Freda was close to her sister and her mother. As she became more depressed she began to rely on them for help, and she also turned to her other friends for emotional support. She didn't want to burden Mel because he had his own problems. Besides, he had never liked to talk much about feelings. While Freda's circle of support gave her the help she needed, it also caused her to pull away more and more from Mel, and he was left with no one. Except for his wife, he had no one in his life who really cared about him and to whom he could talk.

I would like to think that Mel is an isolated case of a man who is so cut off from his own feelings and support from others that he thinks of ending his life when he gets depressed. However, many men are in peril because of the lack of intimate, meaningful relationships in their lives.

CAREGIVING

Men are caretakers; women are caregivers. In study after study, the gender differences in caregiving are distinct. Women are the primary caregivers for children, for spouses, and for parents. Men may provide help on a schedule, but women are usually on call for all these people twenty-four hours a day, seven days a week. I can't remember ever hearing a mother say that she is babysitting her own children, but it is not uncommon for both people to consider the father as babysitting when the mother has to be gone from home. The same dynamics occur in the care of elderly parents. The son or son-in-law often helps out by doing home maintenance or keeping up the checkbook—things that he can do in the evenings or on the weekends. But the daughter or daughter-in-law is called on for the bed and body work of ailing mothers and fathers at any time of the day or night. The caregiving responsibilities of women are thus often much more demanding, time-consuming, and intimate than those of men.

Much of the gender difference in caregiving comes from imposed societal roles, but many women report that these caregiving relationships are very meaningful and give them great satisfaction even at times when they are burdensome and stressful. Men are missing out on some of the most intimate relationships that can ever be experienced by taking care only of the business end of the caregiving needs that occur in families. Those men who do become involved in the intimacy of caregiving roles often find new aspects of themselves that they never knew existed.

Freddie had always been a gentle man. In fact, some might say that his wife, Maude, was the decision maker and the dominant one in their family. When she became terminally ill, he did not hesitate to take care of her. Their three children all lived in other parts of the country and were not available to help out. Some of the people from the church dropped by from time to time and the neighbors checked on him every day, but he had to take over all the things that she used to do and take care of her, too. The children were worried that such caregiving duties were going to be too much for him, and they pleaded with him to move closer to one of them so that they could take over, but he refused.

While Maude was still able she taught him how to make their favorite recipes. She showed him how to work the washing machine and sort the clothes. Soon she was no longer able to do any of the housework and then even needed his help in bathing and dressing. They hired a housekeeper, but all the other tasks of caregiving were Freddie's and he found that he really enjoyed being in charge of the house and of his wife's care. When she became very ill and needed a nurse for part of each day, Freddie joined a local caregiving support group. The other members were all women, but they welcomed him and gave him a lot of pointers on how to do his job better. By the time Maude died, he had made many new friends in the group and was deeply grateful that he had faced the challenge of taking care of his wife and had succeeded at something that no one thought he could do. He knew that Maude would have taken care of him if he needed it, and he was proud that he had been able to do the same for her.

Freddie is an example of a man open to learning women's ways of doing things, first from his wife, then from the women in the support group. He's a strong man in that he resisted his children's efforts to take charge of his wife's care, but he was humble and admitted that he needed help in learning how to be a caregiver. His own chances for survival, now that his wife has died, are improved because of the new skills and the many friends and resources he gained during his caregiving experience.

SUPPORT SYSTEMS

Because women are the caregivers, because women seek help when they need it, because women learn to build intimate, close, reciprocal relationships, women end up their lives with much better support systems than do men. Men's lifestyles not only put them at risk for earlier death but also at risk of having no support in late life. Relationships with adult children are crucial in old age. Men who have been workaholics, alcoholics, or absent fathers do not have the relationships with family that would serve them when they need someone to depend on. Newspapers sometimes carry stories of an elderly person who has been abandoned by his or her family. The first reaction is to condemn the uncaring children for neglect of their parent, but when the situation is investigated further, there is almost always a history of abuse, neglect, or abandonment on the part of the parent when those children were young.

Most children take care of their parents if needed and are especially caring and responsible for parents who were caring and responsible for them as they were growing up. Children learn how to care and take care of others from those who cared for them. Therefore, both men and women are investing in their own futures by being good, loving caregivers of their children. I have seen very loving care given by children for their parents and have marveled at the wonderful relationships that nurture such care. On the other side, I have encountered very distressing situations in which the abusive or uncaring actions of the parents have come back to haunt them in their old age. Larry was such a man.

After seventy-three-year-old Larry's wife died, his only son moved him to the Midwest and placed him in a nursing home. Larry gave the nursing home staff much difficulty with his cursing and resistance to care. He yelled at his roommate and refused to come out of his room for meals. He was in a wheelchair, with both legs bandaged because of circulation problems from diabetes. His doctor told him that he was going to have to amputate both feet if Larry did not comply with care and show improvement soon.

Larry had lived on the East Coast all his life and had no idea what this small Midwestern town was like or why his son had moved him here. He felt truly lost, and the only people he knew in this new place were his son and daughter-in-law. They rarely visited him. Once they tried to take him home with them for Christmas, but he ended up fighting with them so much that they vowed they would never invite him to their home again. The son stopped paying the nursing home bill regularly and the staff suspected that the son was cashing Larry's Social Security checks for his own use. The administrator was threatening the son with discharge of his father.

In a telephone conversation, the son revealed that his father had been an alcoholic and had been verbally and physically abusive to him as he was growing up. Now, while he didn't want to completely abandon his father, he didn't feel much love or concern for the troubles his father was having, either. He felt that he had done his duty by placing him in a nursing home where he could be cared for but he didn't want to put up with his father's continued verbal abuse every time he tried to visit him. The nursing home took action to get access to Larry's Social Security checks and quit relying on the son for payment. Once that was accomplished, the son quit inquiring about his father's welfare and never visited him again.

Larry missed his wife very much and was frightened about the possible amputation of his feet. He blamed his son for his problems, and he was in despair because he had no one to help him out. A few months later, he died—a lonely, angry, and depressed old man—only days after his feet were amputated.

RELATIONSHIPS AND LONGEVITY

As our society ages and there are more and more older people in need of help, there is increasing concern about the stress that caregiving imposes on the caregivers. Women are the primary caregivers, and they're the ones who are experiencing significant levels of caregiving stress. Women bear the burden of more overt stress in all relationships because they allow themselves to be sensitive to the stress of others in ways that men do not.

By standing apart, ignoring the warning signs of distress, and keeping an objective perspective on their relationships, shock-absorbing men are able to separate themselves from the intensive emotional impact of close relationships. This enables them to avoid the relationship stress that women often encounter and helps them avoid the stress that others are feeling. These gender differences in social health may account for the greater depression that women experience in youth and middle age. However, in late life those dynamic relationships that women struggle with are extremely crucial for survival. Men, who have separated themselves from relationship stressors, don't have the support systems needed for longevity.

Some people believe that the best investment that people can make toward a long and happy life is to make sure they have wives or daughters who will take care of them in old age. Heterosexual women don't have the advantage of having women partners to take care of them, so if they have no daughters they must hope for husbands who have learned new ways of relating and who are learning feminine qualities of caregiving as well as masculine methods of caretaking.

We often think about the need for money in old age, and I don't discount the importance of financial resources. But I've seen very poor people with loving families who enjoy a high quality of life and who look forward to a very happy old age. I have also seen wealthy people without family or friends who have the highest quality of medical care but a very low quality of life. They're bitter about the past and hopeless about the future. Even though they have everything that money can buy to make their lives comfortable, their lives are miserable. They lack good social health. This has convinced me that we all need to put at least as much time into building good relationships as we put into building lucrative careers, so that we have good social support and loving care as well as financial resources in our retirement years.

CHAPTER SEVEN

Occupational Health:

Our Roles, Ourselves

⟡

P roductive work, whether at home, in a paid job, or in a volunteer role, is important to our sense of worth and well-being throughout life. Too many men work productively up until the time of their retirement and then become extremely unhappy with too much time on their hands and nothing to do. They lose a sense of themselves and their role in life when they no longer work at their jobs. Some even become ill and die within months or a few years after retirement. For most of us, life isn't worth living if we don't feel like we're making a contribution to society in some meaningful way. Our work is how we fulfill that need.

Occupational health has become much more complex for women in the past fifty years as they have more work roles than ever before. Along with increased responsibilities have come greater life satisfaction, increased stress, and better economic resources in old age for women. Men's work roles have not changed so dramatically. There is an old saying, "A man works from sun to sun, but a woman's work is never done." Most women agree with this statement wholeheartedly, especially those with multiple roles of caregiver, mother, homemaker, breadwinner, and wife. While these multiple roles and never-ending jobs are stressful for women, they serve to give women many options in the way they define themselves occupationally. They can give up one role but continue on in other familiar roles throughout their lives. Women have the advantage of role continuity. Men tend to define their occupational roles around their paid work, but women rarely identify themselves only as a paid worker. Thus a woman's work is round the clock and a man's work is considered over when he punches out on the time clock. Of course, most men work around the house and take some responsibility for their children, but those jobs are not how they think of themselves in their occupational roles.

Another major factor in occupational health is the economics of work. Is our work valued enough by society that we are paid for our efforts? Men usually get paid for their work, but women engaged in traditional work are either unpaid or earn very low pay. As a result, men have historically had the economic advantage in occupational roles—their roles have been valued more by society. To maintain their self-esteem over the life span, women have had to define the value of the work they do in terms of things other than money. This disparity leaves women at a disadvantage when it comes to economic resources, but at an advantage when it comes to internal resources and resilience to cope with changing roles in old age.

ROLE IDENTITY

In many ways, our work is key to our identity, self-esteem, and well-being. If we limit ourselves to a narrow definition of work, we limit our sense of self as well. In contrast, if we realize that our work roles can be many and varied, then we are able to think of ourselves as worthwhile, productive, and engaged with life in a much broader context.

As women break the bonds of restrictive sex roles, they are expanding their views of their worth. Men are having a difficult time with change because as women redefine their work roles, men's roles are challenged. Some men respond to these developments by attempting to force women back into old roles. Susan Faludi, in *Backlash: The Undeclared War Against American Women,* describes this dynamic very well.

> That women have in their possession a vast and untapped vitality also
> explains one of the more baffling phenomena of the backlash—the

seeming "overreaction" with which some men have greeted even the tiniest steps toward women's advancement. Maybe these men weren't overreacting after all. In the '80s, male politicians saw the widening gender gap figures. Male policymakers saw the polls indicating huge and rising majorities of women demanding economic equality, reproductive freedom, a real participation in the political process, as well as a real governmental investment in social services and a real commitment to peace. . . . Male corporate heads saw the massive female consensus for child care and family leave policies and the vast female resentment over indecent pay and minimal promotions. Male evangelical leaders saw the huge number of "traditional" wives who were ignoring their teachings or heading for the office. All of these men understood the profound force that an American women's movement could exert if it got half a chance [p. 459].

In essence, as women are enhancing their economic worth and well-being, men are struggling with an identity crisis because they don't know how to think of themselves as masculine men if women are functioning in the same occupational roles. As women have moved forward, many men feel they're losing ground—and along with that, they're losing their place in society. Most men have not yet discovered that their work and worth can and should expand beyond the workplace and into family, community, and volunteer roles, places that have been the domains of women.

Ask a modern woman who she is or what she does and she will usually describe many more roles than only her official occupation outside the home. Men, however, typically describe themselves only by the work they perform for pay. "I'm an engineer." "I'm a lawyer." "I'm a professor." "I'm a salesman."

I have observed such gender differences in occupational identity through my work as a conference planner. For a long time, I have organized conferences where I come into contact with nationally known experts in the field of gerontology and psychology. In the course of gathering material for publicity and spending time with these speakers, I get to know quite a bit about their lives. Inevitably, I learn much more about the women—about their families and interests outside their area of expertise—than I learn about the men. The men tend to be much more focused on their professional life and usually do not reveal much about their family life, their volunteer work, or their leisure interests. The men talk about the research they are doing, the colleagues they associate with, and their theories and practices.

The women speakers, by contrast, talk about their lives in a much broader context. While they certainly present their professional expertise, they also include information about their families and their avocations in conversations and even on printed biographical materials. By the time a conference is over, I usually know if the women are married, how many children and grandchildren they have, what their hobbies are, and much more about each of them as a whole person than I do about most of the men speakers.

This is not to say that men don't value the many roles in their lives or that they are reluctant to talk about these other things. They just aren't as likely to mix their professional roles with their personal and private roles, and their professional roles are their major source of identity in the world.

Such overidentification with paid work makes men vulnerable when they retire because they lose a major sense of themselves. When they give up the work role, they are at a loss as to how to define themselves once they are no longer an engineer, a lawyer, a professor, or a salesman.

TRADITIONAL OCCUPATIONAL ROLES

As the traditional family breadwinners, men have long been thought of as the laborers outside the home. And women, as family nurturers, have traditionally been thought of as the housekeepers, cooks, and caregivers in the home. Men have been expected to work around the house doing yard work and home maintenance on weekends, but much of the literature from the first half of the century and even into the 1960s and 1970s emphasizes the importance of a home as a sanctuary for a man, a place of rest and relaxation away from the stresses of work. The woman has been responsible for providing such a sanctuary for her man, with warm, tasty meals, a clean house, and obedient children waiting for him when he arrives home from work each day.

This view of women's work was emphasized after the Second World War, when women were encouraged to return from the factories and offices to make homes for the men returning from the war. Most adults remember television shows such as *Father Knows Best* and *Leave It to Beaver,* which promoted these views of the family. Popular magazines like *Better Homes and Gardens, Redbook, Woman's Day,* and

Family Circle were heavily displayed at every checkout line in every grocery store. They're still featured at checkout stands today—but so are *New Woman, Self,* and other health and fitness magazines, as well as the popular tabloids like the *National Enquirer,* that present very different views of life's possibilities.

Of course, most traditional media images have presented views of the middle-class white family in traditional marriages. For many, especially for low-income ethnic minorities, such compartmentalized family life was rarely possible. Many low-income women have always had to work outside the home for low wages and few benefits whether they wanted to or not.

While it's been hard for women to gain access to men's work, it isn't easy for men to expand their roles into women's work, either. Our society doesn't provide rewards for child care and housework, in money or respect and recognition. These important responsibilities are viewed as menial, low-status work. It is no wonder that men haven't rushed to take over such responsibilities as women have entered the workplace. Who would want to add the pressures of low-status and unpaid menial work to their occupational identities? Those men who have attempted to get involved in the work of family and home are often looked down on by others as less masculine and lacking ambition.

In addition to the stigma that men feel in taking on what they think of as "women's work," many women have been reluctant to give up or share control of their core role as nurturer and homemaker. For much of history, women's only source of power has been the home. The way it looks, the way it functions, and the way it is managed, along with the control of the children, have been the major areas in life where women have been in charge. While they often have felt burdened by the criticism and blame for a less-than-perfect house or the bad behavior of their children, they also have felt fulfilled and proud to see the house run smoothly and the children grow up successfully.

Such power dynamics between husband and wife become especially apparent at the time of retirement. Women who have been running households for decades rarely welcome the efforts of retired husbands to try to change the way their wives spend their time.

"He's driving me nuts!" said Melba, the wife of recently retired Joe, a former accountant. "He insists on helping me in the kitchen, and then he puts things back in weird places where I can't find them. His help is more trouble than it's worth."

"I just think that there are better ways to organize the dishes and the pots and pans, but she is so set on having things in the kitchen her way that she gets furious when I get things out of order," explains Joe. "It seems to me that if I help her with the housework, then we'll have more time to do things together."

Joe and Melba weren't prepared in practical ways for his retirement. She had her established ways of doing her work and conducting her life. Now that he has retired, he expected that she would change her work so that they could be together more. To him, that meant that he would share in household tasks and that she would do things with him. She hadn't thought of his retirement meaning that she had to retire from her life, too. She liked her life as it had been. She enjoyed her volunteer work, her lunches with friends, her time to watch the soaps on television, her time to garden and read. Now, he wanted her to give all that up—or at least to rearrange everything around his interests, his plans, and his retirement.

He wanted her devotion and attention. She wanted him to find something to do to replace his job and to let her have her life back.

In retirement, Joe has no work to do—but Melba's work continues much as it has been all her life. She knows her role and its worth. He has no work role any longer and begins feeling useless. This can lead to depression and despair if he doesn't find a substitute role, but without the life experience of multiple roles he has nothing to fall back on.

BREAKING THE BONDS
OF TRADITIONAL ROLES

As women take on jobs outside the home, they don't have to give up their core occupations as family nurturers and household managers. They just add on new occupational roles. The term *supermom* has become a part of our language and everyone knows what it means— a woman who is juggling many, many roles and responsibilities. *Superdad* has not become a common word because men have not kept up with women in increasing their occupational identities. Men's occupations remain primarily outside the home in one or maybe two paid jobs. Men are not as likely to think of their roles as husbands, fathers, and househusbands as meaningful occupational roles in their lives.

Multiple Roles

Just as we need flexibility in physical, emotional, and social health, we also need flexibility in occupational health. The more ways in which we identify ourselves as contributing members of society and as productive human beings, the more options we have to fall back on if and when we lose one of our occupational roles. When women view themselves only as wives and mothers, they suffer role loss to a much greater extent with divorce, widowhood, and the empty nest than do women who have a career, paid employment outside the home, or meaningful volunteer work. Likewise, men who identify only with their jobs are lost without that role, whether they get downsized, fired, or retired.

As I discussed in the chapter on mental health, women's depression seems to peak in midlife when the roles of mother and homemaker are in transition with the children leaving home. Hormones do influence the menopausal years for women—but the shift in a woman's occupational roles during those years is also a significant influence on her health and well-being. Likewise, men's depression increases with age. It tends to peak after the age of sixty-five when they are no longer employed and must search for new ways in which to define their worth.

The good news is that women have been rapidly increasing their occupational options and are much less at risk of despair with the loss of the core responsibilities of wife and mother. Now that they are working outside the home and are involved in responsible volunteer work, they're not so bereft when homemaking responsibilities diminish or disappear from their lives. In addition, their roles as caregivers are now extending well past sixty-five with the responsibilities of parent and spousal care and, more recently, with the need to take on primary caregiving roles for grandchildren whose parents are unable to care for them. Whether these multiple roles are seen as blessings or burdens, women are rarely left feeling that they are not needed somewhere by someone. And while they don't have the economic resources that men do, most women are usually able to occupy themselves in satisfying ways throughout their lives.

Men, by contrast, haven't expanded their roles in life as well as women. Although women have gone out into the workplace in the past few decades, most men haven't come into the homes or become involved in volunteer work to increase their occupational identities. Our society has programmed them to be successful by staying in one occupational role and focusing on advancement through dedication, hard work, and long hours. The reward for such behavior is supposed to be retirement in which they can suddenly be free from stress and pressure with enough money to enjoy life. Men don't learn to find meaning in work outside paid employment. When they get that gold watch, they suddenly discover that they no longer feel important to anyone. Time lies heavy on their hands.

Hal had been part of a very successful family business. Along with his father, his brothers, and his brothers-in-law, he built a small grocery business into a large food distribution corporation. He worked long hours and had no time to get involved in family activities or any other outside interests. He loved his work and took pride in the fact that everyone in town knew his name and knew that he provided extremely well for his family. He donated to worthy causes as part of his obligation to the welfare of others. Because of such generosity, the town had named a park after his family, recognizing them as major contributors to the community.

With the rapid growth of supermarket chains, Hal's business began to fail—it could not keep up with such major competition. In addition, the next generation of children were not interested in working in the family business, so with the death of Hal's father, the brothers agreed that it was time to sell the business and to retire. Hal was then sixty-three years old and in good health. He didn't know what he would do next but knew that he would have plenty of money to travel and to enjoy himself for the first time in his life. He didn't realize how much the business and his job were central to his feelings of worth and well-being. He was not prepared for what was to come.

At first, Hal and his wife, Beth, took several trips they had looked forward to. Then when they returned home, Beth went back to her activities in a theater group and her church. She also began volunteer teaching. Hal felt bored and unsure about what he could do with his time. He began to go by his old office to visit with the new owners— but it wasn't the same. He came home upset at the changes they were making in what had been his business. His kids were all involved with their own lives and their families. His grandchildren would come by but he didn't have much interest in playing ball or children's games with the little ones and the teenagers had nothing in common with him.

He began going for long walks in the woods and thinking about how meaningless his life had become. Nobody needed him anymore.

Nobody had time for him or even any interest in him. In fact, he knew he wasn't a very interesting person and he felt no one would really miss him if he were out of the picture. Several times, when he was alone in the woods, he would become overwhelmed with thoughts of just lying down and merging with the earth and nature. He began to think of how he could commit suicide. Fortunately, he got scared enough by such thoughts to talk to his wife about his feelings. She insisted that he seek help in dealing with the occupational crisis that retirement had brought on.

Hal's experience is not uncommon among men who have devoted their entire lives to their occupations. Many men today are experiencing such crises much earlier in life due to the downsizing of large corporations. Men who have worked hard to get ahead in their companies are being laid off or forced to retire long before they're ready or prepared to face life without work. If they don't find new roles and meaningful activities, they live out their lives in boredom, despair, or illness. Some turn to drugs or alcohol. Some are victims of heart attacks or cancer and lose the motivation or will to fight their diseases. Some take their own lives. For many, however, such an occupational crisis early in their lives will cause them to take stock of what is important. Men who find ways other than paid employment to feel worthwhile and fulfilled will be much busier and much happier in their old age than they can be with nothing but memories of their former function to sustain them.

Continuity of Work Roles

Men and women who are engaged with life in their old age are often people who have never quit working or who constantly find satisfaction in the new roles that they assume after retirement. Work that involves creativity, caregiving, or new challenges is crucial to living a long and productive life. Gerontologist Sheldon Tobin once told me that he had found two types of people who are never ready to die: artists and parents of developmentally disabled children. Artists feel that they are always on the cusp of a new discovery and parents of developmentally disabled children never feel finished with their caregiving role.

Teachers and ministers are two other occupational roles that I've noticed among people who are living well in old age in the retirement centers I visit. The teachers continue to be interested in the learning process for themselves and for others and the ministers are interested in reaching out and assisting in the spiritual needs of others. Richard, for example, continues to minister to others long after his official retirement.

> Eighty-year-old Richard says, "I'm busier now that I've moved into the retirement center than I ever was before I left my job as a minister." He spends his days visiting people in the nursing home and the hospital. Such visitations were something that he never had enough time for when he was the minister of a large church in the Midwest. After retirement, he has felt relieved that he is no longer burdened with the administrative business of his lifelong work and can now spend as much time as he pleases in doing what he had always enjoyed most, bringing comfort to people who are sick. The people in the nursing homes look forward to his visits, and he knows that his life has meaning to others in very significant ways. It doesn't matter to him that he no longer gets paid for doing this work. His work has always been central to his life and he sees no reason to quit now. As long as he is able, he will continue his life's mission as a volunteer. In fact, as a volunteer, he is finding new freedom to do the work he loves on his own schedule without worrying about having to answer to anyone else.

New Occupational Roles

Some people have not wanted to continue on in the same work they did while employed. They take on new projects and jobs that they didn't have time for at earlier periods in their lives.

> "I always knew I was a writer," says Marge. At age sixty-five, she began writing short stories and articles and sending them to newsletters and magazines. "I hate the rejections, but when I get something published, even in an obscure newsletter, I feel renewed and wonderful," she exclaims. After long years of working as a secretary at a university, she had watched professors publish articles and books. It had always been her secret dream to try her own hand at writing, but she never had the time while she was working and raising her family. "Now, I get up each morning and go to my computer and begin to write. It's more fun than work and the time just flies. Next I plan to take a course on writing poetry and try my hand at that!"

Though caregiving of the elderly is often thought of as a burden, for some it is a task of joy and fulfillment. Gertrude has found her calling after working many years as a custodian.

"My work cleaning office buildings was a way to make a living," says sixty-year-old Gertrude, "but it was only a job. Since I've become certified as a nurse's aide, I feel that I have a job that is so much more. It thrills me to be able to bring comfort and a little bit of happiness to these old people who have so little time left in their lives." She dreamed of becoming a nurse when she was a little girl, but she got pregnant and had to get married before she finished high school. Later, as a single parent, she had to find a job that would pay the most and would fit her time schedule. She could work as a custodian at night while the kids were asleep and be there to get them off to school when they woke up in the morning. She forgot about her dream to be a nurse even after her children were grown, until a friend got a job in a nursing home. Through her friend, Gertrude learned that she could be certified as a nurse's aide and could easily get a job in the health care profession.

At first, it seemed foolish to give up her custodian job, which was secure and which paid fairly decent wages after twenty years, but she decided that if she was ever going to follow her dream she had better do it now. "And I haven't regretted it for a minute," she adds.

In late life, when old work roles are no longer available, occupational health depends on having other meaningful roles to pursue. Women have more experience than men in juggling many roles and in switching from one role to another at different times in their lives. I often warn younger men that they need to learn women's work for their own survival. Men who learn to be nurturing caregivers and homemakers are taking care of their own interests for finding meaning and for staying independent in their old age as much or more than they are being helpful to their wives.

Gender differences in late life show that, though women report many more functional disabilities than men in old age, many more women live alone and are able to take care of themselves. One reason why men find it necessary to remarry soon after they become widowers is that they don't have the skills to take care of themselves. If they have never learned the art of homemaking or of making friends, they are extremely dependent on women when their wives die. After retirement, the primary occupational goals are effective homemaking and engagement in meaningful activities and relationships. The person with a history of participation in multiple roles has a much better chance of meeting these occupational goals than the single-minded specialist.

THE ECONOMICS OF OCCUPATIONAL HEALTH

If there is any one area of life where men clearly have advantages over women, it's in the financial and economic arena. Most of women's work hasn't been valued enough to be rewarded with pay. As a result, women who have labored all their lives are ending up living longer but poorer than men. It has been observed that if women's economic resources were equal to men's, they would be living even longer and with a much higher quality of life than they now experience.

Older women today are suffering greatly because they haven't had histories of earning money in their own right. They're dependent on whatever pensions or retirement benefits their husbands' work might afford them. These older women are often dependent entirely on a very low fixed income from Social Security benefits. If a couple did manage to save money for their old age, the husband's illnesses often use it up—he is usually the partner who becomes ill and dies first. This leaves the wife in these situations without any remaining benefit from a lifetime of hard work and saving for the future. Fifteen percent of all women over sixty-five years old are now living below the poverty line—and the figures for women of color are much greater. One-half of all black women over sixty-five who live alone are impoverished.

In earlier times, women had to choose between marriage and a career. Few women had the option to have both. The older women who chose careers may or may not be ending their lives with regrets about their decisions to stay single, but they're certainly living better economically than many women who made the choice for marriage. Retirement centers around the country are filled with older people who are able to afford living arrangements that provide nice surroundings, social activities, and supportive professional care as they need it. Invariably in these retirement centers I meet dynamic women who were never married and who lived their lives as professional career women.

Many were teachers. Others worked in government jobs. A few have been nurses. These professions were the ones most apt to have provided retirement benefits sufficient to enable women to live relatively comfortably and well in their advanced years. These women have always been in complete control of their economic lives and have no difficulty understanding and managing their finances in their old age. Women who have been married and are now widowed seem to have more concerns about their finances. Sometimes it's because they do have very limited means; other times it's because they have never learned to manage money and feel insecure about their abilities in this area. If they've never learned to manage their own financial affairs, they become dependent on others to take over this important part of their lives after their husbands die. Sometimes it's one of their children (typically a son) who takes on the job, or a professional money manager such as a bank trustee. In any event, women who've never learned money management often become anxious about their financial well-being in late life whether they need to be or not.

Penelope is an example of an independent career woman who continues to be in charge of her finances in old age.

"I've always been an independent thinker and I didn't want any man telling me how I should live my life or manage my affairs!" says eighty-five-year-old Penelope. "Sometimes I regret that I didn't have children, but my life as a teacher has given me hundreds of children, and many of them continue to send me letters and cards even though they are now grandparents themselves." Penelope (who insists that all young people call her Miss Smith) lives in a nursing home since her health has worsened and she had to move from her apartment at the adjoining retirement center. She lived in that apartment for many years with her only sister, who was widowed and needed a place to live and a companion. Penelope took her in until her death. Now her only remaining relative is her sister's son, who lives across the country. She feels close to her nephew and keeps him informed about her business affairs because he'll be her sole heir, but she would never consider turning her finances over to him to manage unless she had no other choice. "Why would I let anyone else take care of my business?" she exclaims, when it was suggested to her that she should give someone her power of attorney or appoint a guardian because of her age. "I'm sure that he would do it and would do a fine job, but I wouldn't feel comfortable about my security if I weren't managing my own affairs. This way I know how much I have and how much I can afford to spend. I've never had to go to anyone else to get access to my own money and I don't intend to start at this late date."

Dorothy (introduced in previous chapters) feels much the same way, although she lives below the poverty line on a fixed Social Security income.

"I had to scrimp and save throughout my life to make ends meet, so it's not that much different now," says eighty-one-year-old Dorothy. "My family was always poor. My father was often out of work, and my mother always bought our clothes at rummage sales. I can't eat oatmeal to this day because I had to eat it morning, noon, and night during the Depression years. Thank goodness for Social Security. I don't know what I would do without it and without subsidized housing for senior citizens. I had very little retirement benefits when I was forced to retire from my retail sales job at age sixty-two. I'd worked in factories and sales most of my life for low pay and no benefits, and I was divorced at age thirty-one, so when I had to retire, I was totally dependent on Social Security. Since my pay was so low, I only qualified for a very low monthly check, but it is better than being out on the street. I manage to get by just like I learned to when I was little."

With the women's movement for equality, the working women of today will not only have better benefits and resources in their old age, they'll have experience in money management as well. Many women who work outside the home now are beginning to accumulate some funds toward retirement in their own name and for their own use. Though women continue to make lower salaries than men, at least now many more are receiving salaries and will be able to reap some benefits from their labors for their old age.

ECONOMIC RESOURCES, ROLE CONTINUITY, AND LONGEVITY

Occupational health is a mixed bag as far as gender differences go. Women seem to have the advantage over men in that they've made much progress in expanding their occupational role identities. In the past, when women identified only with being housewives and mothers, they often felt worthless and unproductive after midlife when their families were grown. Now, in spite of the difficulties and stresses of being supermoms and juggling multiple responsibilities, women have many roles in their lives that give them numerous options for occupational health and well-being. A woman rarely retires from all her roles, so she can feel a sense of role continuity throughout life with caregiving, hobbies, and volunteer work, as well as with paid employment.

Men haven't yet realized solid role continuity after retirement. Their work identities continue to be closely tied to their paid employment, which leads to problems in later life. After men retire, they often don't recognize the productivity, contribution, and value that family-oriented caregiving roles and volunteer work could bring to their sense of occupational well-being. They need more experience in these work roles in their younger years to appreciate their value in later life, after they are no longer working in paid employment. But until such unpaid endeavors are recognized as valuable to our society, I fear that men will be resistant to dedicated participation in caregiving and volunteer work.

Men have the advantage of economic resources as a result of occupational work outside the home. They're paid more than women and they accumulate more benefits for later life in the form of savings and pensions. Without Medicare and Social Security benefits, many older people, especially women, would be in dire circumstances because they haven't had the opportunity of paid employment that provides retirement benefits. The women's movement for equality in the workplace has begun to turn this trend around, and future generations of women will have financial resources in their old age that should begin to provide for an improved quality of life.

Both economic resources and role continuity are important to longevity. Good health care and safe living conditions are the things that money can buy. Without enough economic resources to have adequate shelter and health care or without a feeling of worth and productivity, both men and women can lose the will to live.

CHAPTER EIGHT

Spiritual and Environmental Health:
Ourselves in Context

─∿∿─

Although the spiritual dimension of life is important to a great many people, it has been neglected as an area of research and study until very recently. For some, spiritual health centers around religious belief, but for others it takes on a much broader context and incorporates all the things that give meaning and purpose to life. Spirituality connects us to our deepest internal personal feelings and beliefs, to our creativity, and to the broadest concepts of universal truth. It also connects us with all that has preceded our birth and all that is to follow our death. The traditions we inherit from our ancestors to guide us through life and the legacies we hope to leave for our progeny all contribute to our spiritual wellness.

While the spiritual dimension of wellness refers to internal beliefs and processes, the environmental dimension refers to the external context in which we live our lives. Our external surroundings provide the climate that stimulates health or illness in the physical, mental, social, occupational, and spiritual aspects of our lives. Environmental health is thus both directly and indirectly important to longevity. If the place in which we live is safe and nourishing, then we'll find it relatively easy to maintain our health, but if it's barren, polluted, dangerous, or hostile, our health and ultimately our lives are threatened.

THE SPIRITUAL DIMENSION

As people age, they develop greater *interiority*. This word has been coined by gerontologists to describe increased internalization of past, recent, and new experiences. This doesn't mean that older people withdraw from others and become introverted, it simply means that they spend time reflecting on the past and seeking understanding, meaning, and purpose in life. Those who develop interiority in a positive way trust themselves to determine if something is good, worthwhile, or satisfying rather than looking outside themselves for validation.

Erik Erikson, a well-known developmental psychologist, called this the need for "ego integrity." He believed that those people who do not achieve ego integrity end their lives in despair. They're not able to look back over their lives and find satisfaction. They're the people who reach old age and say, "I didn't make a difference" or "Life has no meaning" or "This world would have been a better place if I had never lived."

Men and women who live longest appear to be those with ego integrity, positive interiority, and optimism for the future. They continue to have hope and to find satisfaction, meaning, and purpose in whatever they do, no matter how aged, disabled, or limited they become. They create nurturing, caring environments for themselves and continue to do so for others as long as they're able. They're engaged with life in deeper, more meaningful ways than when they were younger. They feel ready for death but are satisfied with living. They know that they will be remembered by others after they are gone.

Edna is an example of someone who is living in excellent spiritual and environmental health in extreme old age.

One-hundred-year-old Edna delights in sitting in the sun on the porch of the retirement center. She can no longer hear and her vision is limited—but she can feel the warmth of the sun on her face and she is glad to be alive to experience the beauty of the outdoors. She has five children, many more grandchildren, and even more great-grandchildren. She loves to think about her past, to remember when her children were growing up, and to fantasize about how her great-grandchildren will become good and important people. She wants them to know and remember her after her death. She thinks about and plans for the legacies she will leave.

She welcomes companionship from any visitors or other residents who stop by to say, "Hello," or to sit with her for a while, but she is equally content with solitude. She truly lives in the moment and has reached a state of acceptance and appreciation of herself, her life, the world, and others around her. She doesn't keep up with the news any longer, but she stays attentive to what's happening in her own world. She's an inspiration to everyone who knows her.

Edna is reaching the end of life with great satisfaction and pleasure. She enjoys her surroundings and is connected to nature and people, but, at the same time, is at peace with her solitude.

While spiritual and environmental dimensions are important at all stages of life, they become extremely important to wellness in late life when other life dimensions may become compromised. For those who have lived well beyond the average life expectancy, physical health is often tenuous. As the body slows down, so do all other aspects of life, so that things that once seemed important to study and worry about may seem trivial or dull in advanced years. When people reach their nineties and beyond, they've typically outlived most of their significant relationships, including not only their parents, spouses, siblings, and friends, but even their doctors, lawyers, and ministers, and perhaps some of their children. They now must rely on their own internal resources for sustenance and meaning. Their environmental space is reduced, and they spend increasing amounts of time alone.

Contrary to popular belief, however, people don't suddenly become more religious as they age. They usually try to maintain levels of religious involvement that they had in earlier life. If church attendance was a part of their life in younger years, they'll want to continue to attend religious services in their later life, but if they weren't active in religion prior to old age, most people don't find it important in later years, either.

GENDER AND RELIGION

Women are clearly more religious than men at all stages of life. Women attend church, pray, read religious materials, and participate in religious activities more often than men. This is especially true for the middle-aged and older women in our society today. It appears that since many women have been shut out from jobs and educational opportunities, some turn to religious activities to give meaning to their lives and for personal satisfaction outside their families. The church has been the center of their social activities. When older women live alone, the church may be their primary resource for love and affection. As one elder woman once told me, "I go to church to get hugged and kissed."

Researchers find that women have more intrinsic or internal, personal religious beliefs, while men have more extrinsic or external, impersonal reasons for being religious. Women find their religious beliefs give them avenues for personal growth, to become better people, to help others. Men find religion a source of comfort and social benefit. They go to church to make contacts, gain leadership roles, and to be seen as good parents and family men.

These sex differences in attitudes about religion are seen when young men in their adolescent years leave the church, but then return after they have become settled into a job and have a family. Young women are more likely to stay involved throughout life and are not as apt to leave the church during their youth. If women do decide to reject the church, they rarely return to the fold at a later time as men do. Women's reasons for leaving appear to be deeply personal and less often a casual, youthful, phase-of-life rejection.

As in the corporate world and academia, religious organizations have been and continue to be controlled by men. The leadership of most churches is male dominated, with women taking subordinate roles. This may explain women's more personal, intrinsic religious beliefs—they have not been included in the external benefits of leadership and power that church membership brings to men and have thus found alternative benefits that serve them well in old age.

As women are entering jobs and going to school in greater numbers, their religious activities are decreasing, so that sex differences in religious behaviors like church attendance are also decreasing. While some people believe that women have less time to participate in religious activities once they work or go to school, another reason for the changes in women's religious involvement may be that there are now more avenues open to women for gaining meaning and purpose in their lives, so religion becomes less important.

In old age, when occupational roles have diminished, physical health may be declining, and friends and family members have died, spiritual and religious connections provide motivation and hope for many elders—outlooks that promote longevity. Susie had a long history of work and intellectual activity, but she finds religion to be a source of great strength for her later years.

Susie is an eighty-three-year-old woman who was a teacher in her professional life and who continues to teach Sunday School in her church. She lived at home with her parents until she was married in her forties. Though she was a "Depression kid," she managed to attend college and complete both an undergraduate and a master's degree. She had no children, both of her parents have died, and she has been widowed for thirty years. She lives alone in the house that she and her husband designed and built during their thirteen-year marriage.

Her home is alive with hobbies and activities. She makes quilts, beautifully handcrafted quilts, that are expressions of her creative spirit. Though she usually can't bear to part with the quilts she's made, she often makes special quilts as gifts to bestow on the people she cares about. At Christmas, she decorates her house with a collection of ceramic houses, buildings, and other miniature accessories that she sets up to replicate an old-fashioned village. She arranges the small Christmas village in her living room and invites guests to come and enjoy this display with her. Every year she adds a new piece to her collection so that the village continues to expand, change, and grow.

Susie is a deeply religious woman and has always been active in her church. She names one of the former pastors as the most influential person in her life. She was especially inspired by his unique sense of humor, "He had a joke for every occasion," she recalls. And fun and laughter are the things to which she attributes her own well-being and longevity. "I never grew up—there's a kid in me always wanting to get out. I can have fun when it really isn't a fun place. I can't be sorrowful all the time."

Recently, Susie's physician explained that, although it was time for her periodic medical exams, she might not want to go through such strenuous tests, suggesting that they might be a waste of time because she probably wouldn't be living much longer. She said, without hesitation, "If I'm going to make it to ninety-five, as I intend to, then I better do everything I can to make sure that happens. I'll take the tests!"

Susie is a well-educated career woman who has lived a long life, and her positive, optimistic spirit keeps her involved, inspired, and connected to others. As she suffers physical illness and loses more friends and family members, she may feel depressed at times but she appears to have inner resources that will buffer her against despair and will help her through the inevitable difficulties of old age.

For women living alone in their old age, as so many do, spiritual health is vital to longevity. For many, spirituality means a personal relationship to a higher power, but for others, who may not be religious, spirituality means joyfulness, creative expression, and a strong connection with people, nature, and the environment.

THE ENVIRONMENTAL DIMENSION

How we interact with and control the environment in which we live is very important to holistic health and well-being. Both sexes report equal concern about saving the environment from pollution, nuclear waste, and other contaminants. However, once again, there are gender differences in the ways in which men and women express and act on these concerns. The masculine approach to the environment is to take external action to right the wrongs that are threatening environmental health. Men are more apt to organize and lobby for legislation. Women, by contrast, take a more personal, private approach to protecting the environment and to creating healthy environments in which to live day to day.

As people age, their environmental needs and concerns change because their worlds begin to diminish in size. Young people have the world, even outer space, as options for their lives. They think of wide-ranging travel and of the possibility for living almost anyplace they want. They are mobile and transient. As they mature and begin to settle down in a job with a family, their options and interests become more focused. They become involved with communities and with building dream homes rather than with world and space travel and moving around from here to there. Most people want some roots and a home base from which to live their lives.

After retirement, with the kids out on their own, the family house may become too much bother or too expensive to maintain. Older people, more and more, are moving into smaller and smaller spaces. They go from larger houses to smaller ones, then to apartments or, for those who can afford it, to retirement centers where they live in one-bedroom or efficiency suites with meals, housekeeping, and other services that make life easier. Those who become ill and disabled often end their lives living in one room in a relative's house or a long-term health care institution.

Outsiders tend to see these environmental reductions in space as logical and adaptive. But for older people who are attached to independent homes and lifestyles, moving into smaller and smaller spaces can be disorienting and traumatic. An important ingredient for making these environmental transitions in old age is the ability to ensure meaning and independence throughout the changes. Harry is an example of a man who has successfully maintained his environmental health throughout his long lifetime.

As a young man, Harry was a ranch hand. He loved nature and the outdoor life. He saved money to buy his own land. Eventually he married and settled down on a farm where he had a good life with his wife and children. He worked hard, putting in large crops and harvesting them every year. His success and ability to provide for his family were intricately tied to the natural elements. His sons helped out as they were growing up and one son stayed on as Harry grew older and needed help in the management of the farm. When Harry was in his late sixties, he turned the farm over to his son and devoted himself to tending a large vegetable garden. Though he was no longer directly involved in selling his crops, he was able to provide vegetables for his own table and share them with his family, friends, and neighbors. His wife canned the tomatoes, corn, and beans, and they both won prizes at the state fair every year.

At age eighty, Harry had a stroke. For many months he could only look out the window at the land or sit outside in the sun on fine days. He missed his garden and knew that he would never again be able to put the work into it that it required. But he worked hard at regaining his ability to walk and to use his hands, and as soon as he was able, he began to grow flowers and houseplants. He had window boxes installed on the house, which he filled with beautiful flowers. His home was alive with green and flowering plants. Though he could no longer provide food for the table, he was able to bring beauty to his living environment until the time of his death in his late nineties.

Harry carried his own environmental well-being within him. If he had felt good only while riding the range or harvesting large crops for market, he would have felt lost and hopeless when he could no longer operate the farm. Fortunately, as his world became more contained, he found ways to express his connection to nature in limited environments that were meaningful and satisfying to him and that connected him to others.

I have known many people—mostly women—in their eighties, nineties, and even beyond one hundred, who have a love for nature and who continue to nurture plants in gardens, in boxes, or even in small pots in their rooms at the nursing home. Numerous studies demonstrate that people who care for plants or other living things like pets actually live longer than others in the same circumstances who are not involved in nurturing activities.

A house or apartment filled with healthy plants is a sign of environmental well-being, and so is a place that provides sensory stimulation. Few men seem to have the interest or skills for making a house a home. Most seem to depend on women to provide the sensory stimulation of sights, sounds, and smells in their living quarters. Apart from men's desire for companionship, I believe that this dependence on women to create a healthy living environment is a major reason that widowers remarry soon after they lose a spouse.

In my clinical work and research, I've visited many people in their homes. I'm constantly struck by the barrenness of the living quarters of men (of any age) who live alone. The differences between the environments where women live (whether alone or with a spouse) and those occupied by a single man are striking. Bachelors or widowers tend to have few personal touches in their dwellings. Wall hangings tend to be functional (like a calendar or a clock) or impersonal (like a bulletin board with old, yellowed newspaper articles) but not expressive of the person who lives there (like artwork, children's drawings, or framed family photographs). There are rarely flowers, except for the occasional plastic plants in need of dusting. Women's homes are also full of fragrances from foods cooking on the stove, perfumed sprays, or cleaning materials like floor polish or laundry soap. In single men's homes, sensory stimulation is lacking. There is not as much to look at, to smell, to taste (women almost always offer food), or to touch (stuffed animals, pillows, pets).

I've come to the conclusion that most older men do not have the necessary skills for maintaining environmental health on their own. This leaves them at a disadvantage when they find themselves alone after divorce or the death of a spouse. Not only do they fail to learn how to take care of their personal needs for balanced meals and clean laundry, they suffer from sensory deprivation from such environmental sterility. Women, no matter how limited their resources, more often surround themselves with meaningful and stimulating environments.

Dorothy, the eighty-one-year-old woman introduced in earlier chapters, has arranged her personal environment in a manner typical of many older women I have known.

> Dorothy has made many moves in her life. As a young, divorced working woman with two daughters, she had a small house with a yard big enough for a garden. She fixed up the inside and grew vegetables outside. She worked hard to keep things clean and neat.
>
> After the girls grew up and left home, Dorothy moved to an even smaller house with a large yard. She planted flowers and a strawberry patch. She took care of her houseplants and arranged family photographs throughout her home. She started collecting ceramic owls and soon she had owls peeking out at her from every nook and cranny. Her sewing basket sat beside her recliner and she spent many hours after she retired sitting in her chair, listening to the radio and embroidering pillowcases and dish towels.
>
> In her late seventies, Dorothy became more and more disabled with rheumatoid arthritis. She could no longer tend her flowers and strawberries or travel as she was used to. The yard became too much responsibility, and her hands hurt too much to sew. She decided to sell her house and move into a one-bedroom, subsidized apartment.
>
> Now her living space is even smaller than before. She has no yard and only a few houseplants. Her sewing basket has been replaced with a crossword puzzle book. She tries out new recipes and shares food with her neighbors and her younger sister, who lives around the corner. She takes care of her constant companion, a little fluffy white dog. Family photographs are carefully placed on walls and tabletops, and her owls peek out from everywhere.
>
> As she has become increasingly limited in her mobility, her world has grown smaller. It seems more important than ever before to keep her apartment as comfortable and familiar as possible because that is where she spends most of her time these days.

Many people in nursing homes have gone through processes similar to the one Dorothy is experiencing. The despair that many people feel in nursing homes is as much a result of the environment as it is of their illness. The hospital-like rooms are sterile. The sounds and smells are unfamiliar and even offensive at times. Residents lose privileges that are taken for granted elsewhere, such as freedom to move about, indoors and outdoors, as you please, without having to report your whereabouts to anyone. Such things as privacy to talk on the phone, cry, sing, curse, bathe, go to the bathroom, raid the refrigerator, or even read a book are lost in such institutional settings. Those people in nursing homes who keep their furniture, pictures, pillows, figurines, and other personal items around them enjoy much greater environmental health than those who do not.

LEAVING LEGACIES

Whether or not they have deep spiritual beliefs or environmental concerns, most older adults think about the legacies they will leave behind. The way others will think of us and feel about us after we're gone is an important focus in late life. In fact, a powerful deterrent to suicide in late life is the fear of leaving such a negative memory for others. Though some frail older people may feel ready for death and begin to be hopeless about the future, they somehow find motivation to keep living because they don't want to be remembered as a person who took his or her own life.

In this work-oriented, materialistic society, there is much focus on leaving money as an inheritance for others. Yet that is one of the least satisfying or meaningful legacies that can be left for future generations. People who leave lasting memories of generosity, loving care, mentorship, scholarship, and humor are the ones who make their mark on the future, whether or not they die broke. How many millionaires are remembered for accumulating their fortunes? If they're remembered at all, it's because of their good works, creative inventions, or other achievements—not for their money.

Money may bring comfort, convenience, and good services in old age, but it doesn't ensure satisfaction or spiritual or environmental health. Life is more satisfying and rich for people who leave other kinds of legacies than for those who slave to build a fortune to leave to their heirs. To buy a grandchild a new bike and watch the joy on her face as she learns to ride it is more meaningful than to leave that money to her in a will. To give money to adult children for a down payment on a home that you can visit while you're alive is more satisfying than leaving money for children to build their dream home after you're gone. To take loved ones along with you on trips or excursions gives you joy and keeps your spirit alive for generations to come.

"Die Broke," recommended the title and substance of a recent investment magazine article—that is, spend money on those you love while you're alive, so you get to savor the act of giving and to participate in the joy your generosity creates for others.

Many traditions pass down from generation to generation in ways that are natural and taken for granted by people who are engaged in life at all ages. Spiritually and environmentally healthy people keep traditions alive as part of their legacies to future generations.

Several years ago, my daughter Cynthia and I were delightfully surprised to discover how subtle and strong family tradition can be.

Cynthia needed to go on a business trip when her daughter Emily was only three months old. She asked me to fly out to Colorado and take care of the baby for a few days. I was delighted to spend some time with my new grandbaby. I had been filled with "genetic joy" when she was born and I really looked forward to getting to know her and having her know me.

As soon as I arrived, Cynthia began to give me instructions and to show me lists of things to do, schedules to keep, and emergency numbers to call. It was apparent that she was anxious about leaving her baby. I knew she was thinking, "Is Emily going to be distraught because an unfamiliar person is taking care of her? Will I be doing damage to my baby daughter by leaving her at such an early age?" Though I tried to reassure Cynthia that everything would be okay, I could see that she doubted that I could take care of her baby as well as she could. I was afraid that she might cancel her trip.

In the afternoon when Emily needed a nap, I asked Cynthia to let me take over so she could see that I was perfectly capable of taking care of her baby. As I diapered Emily and rocked her to sleep, Cynthia watched from a distance. I naturally talked baby talk and sang lullabies to my little granddaughter. As I held her in my arms, I was flooded with the memories of holding her mother in much the same way.

After the baby was asleep, Cynthia came to me and said, "Mom, I know now that everything will be all right. As I was listening to you talk and sing to Emily, you were saying the same things and singing the same songs to her that I do. She was happy and comfortable with you. I suddenly remembered that those are the songs that you sang to me when I was a little girl. I had forgotten where I learned them." Some of the songs that I sang to Emily I knew I had learned from my mother and grandmother.

This is an example of how the songs we sing and the ways we treat others pass from generation to generation, even though we don't realize that we are leaving legacies. Women seem to do this naturally—and it's not only babies that benefit from such legacies. I have seen eighty-five- and ninety-year-old women bring much comfort to younger nursing home residents by simply singing old lullabies and hymns to them.

Our nurturing behaviors are legacies we can leave that give meaning to our lives at all ages. Leaving tangible things for others can also be a significant way to connect to others after we are gone.

Lois is dying. She has struggled with a terminal illness for many years, and she knows that the time of her death is getting near. She has little energy left and her eyesight is failing but she is dedicated to her last creative project and is determined to get it finished before she exits from life. She is making beautifully designed, hand-sewn Christmas tree skirts, one for each of her three children and five grandchildren. Each double-sided tree skirt is different and requires intricate crafting and sewing to get all the appliques, beads, and trim attached. She has completed six and is working on the seventh as she talks to me.

"It may seem silly, but I want to be a part of my family's Christmas holidays for years to come. When I accepted the fact that I was not going to beat this illness, I started on this project as a way to be included in family celebrations even after I'm gone. I should've been dead a long time ago, but this gives me a reason to hang on for as long as I can. I know that my kids and grandkids will think of me every year while they decorate their trees."

Older people who are spiritually healthy are involved with creating legacies for their loved ones. They write poetry, books, and letters. They record their life histories or favorite songs and stories for their grandchildren. They get their things in order and clear out the clutter of their lives. They give away meaningful belongings. They want to be remembered as a person who lived a worthwhile life. They want their ideas and their spirits to live on after they are gone.

Ninety-six-year-old Mr. K, a professed agnostic, spent much time in his final years preparing a photograph album for his family. He sorted through boxes of photographs, selecting only a few, which he carefully arranged to represent the separate lineages of himself and his wife. On the left-hand side of the album were pictures of his growing up years with his family and friends and on the right-hand side were his wife's pictures. In the middle of the album were their wedding pictures and then the two sides were united to show their own union. In the back of the album the lineages began to split again as each child left home to form his or her own family.

With the creation of this very special album, Mr. K was able to organize his long life and the life of his wife, who had died many years earlier. The album served as a tribute and a memorial to the good life that they had enjoyed together and to the things they had accomplished.

SPIRITUALITY, ENVIRONMENT, AND LONGEVITY

People who have lost their spiritual well-being or who live in environmental barrenness live without hope and meaning in life. They aren't able to find a sense of joy and humor and they despair. These people tend to die earlier than those who feel good about their past and who are able to live in the present with positive outlook and purpose. People who maintain spiritual and environmental health continue to thrive in spite of chronic illness, poverty, and the other misfortunes that can befall people in their old age.

The ability to live life to its fullest in the face of adversity is apparent in many of the oldest men and women I have come to know over the years. Women seem to have the advantage in spiritual and environmental health because they develop more personal, intrinsic spiritual meaning throughout life and have greater abilities in creating healthy living environments. Men too often depend on women to provide the personal comforts of home and spiritual well-being rather than mastering these dimensions of life themselves. This leaves men at risk if they become isolated and alone. Men and women who develop internalized meaning and purpose in life and honor the legacies they'll leave for others are less vulnerable to feelings of isolation, loneliness, and despair. They accept life as it is and make the very best of it that they can.

Most of the men and women I've met who are more than eighty years of age have few pretenses and are satisfied with simple, basic pleasures. They live in the moment much more than they did when they were younger and are grateful for small things, like good food, a safe home, and people who care about them. They're comfortable talking about death, and they know how they want others to remember them. Younger people are often shocked at how casually older people talk about their own deaths and those of their friends.

My mother tells about a visit with a ninety-nine-year-old friend who said that there were so few of her friends left that no one would show up at her funeral. Her seventy-five-year-old son laughed and said, "Don't worry, Mom. I'll see to it that we serve sandwiches and that will bring a crowd." My mother and her friends enjoy this kind of humor and seem to view funerals and memorial services as a routine part of their lives. Though they're sad about the loss of a relative or friend, they also seem to experience funerals and memorial services as social events where they interact with people they have not seen in a long time.

Spiritually healthy people are able to live fully in the moment, be ready for death at any time, and yet have hope for the future for themselves and for those they will leave behind. All of this is best accomplished within the context of a nurturing environment in which one is safe from harm and stimulated to appreciate the small pleasures and comforts of life. Spiritual and environmental health are important to all the other life dimensions at all ages, but they become crucial to longevity in later life when other dimensions may be in jeopardy. Physical health is often fragile in old age; social health is threatened by the loss of family and friends; occupational health is difficult to maintain when mobility and functional capacities are limited; and mental health is significantly affected by problems in other life dimensions. Strong spiritual and environmental health often keep balance in the wellness system of older women and men at times when all other life dimensions are wavering. Women (in my experience) seem to have developed these deeply personal qualities of life better than men so that they have more spiritual solace and environmental comfort in their final years.

CHAPTER NINE

Living Long and Loving It

T wo growth industries reveal a great deal about the gender differences in our society today. We have populations of older adults and of prisoners who are living in institutions in record numbers, and we need more institutions for both groups every day.

The long-term care industry is building more and more nursing homes to house the multitudes of older people who are living long and needing care. At least two-thirds of these nursing home residents are elder women. On the other hand, we are also building more and more institutions to house aggressive, dangerous, or antisocial people whose behaviors are not acceptable to a civilized community—that is, prisons. Ninety percent of the inmates of these prisons are men. As more and more women are living long and in poor health, more and more men seem to be in need of social control. And though most women and men will never be institutionalized either in nursing homes or in prisons, these disturbing trends are products of our time and represent important gender challenges for the future. Throughout this book, I've pointed out a variety of gender differences in health and aging that are bringing about such phenomena. Now, it's time to discuss what we can do about these differences so that men and women alike may live long, productive, and healthy lives.

CHALLENGES

Unfortunately, living into old age doesn't always mean enjoying life to the fullest. Many women who live long suffer from chronic illness and poverty. Indeed, the few men who do survive into old age are often in better physical health and have more income than their female counterparts. So the challenges for living long and well are not only in helping men stay alive longer but also in helping women live better.

For the past thirty years, the women's movement has been addressing threats to women's health and financial security that keep women from living as well as men. The quality of life for the next generations of older women will undoubtedly improve as a result of these efforts. It is now time for a men's movement, dedicated to those masculine issues in health and longevity that are preventing men from living as long as women.

POWER, PRIVILEGE, AND IMPOTENCE

For men to live longer, they'll need to resist and overcome personal and societal pressures to be macho men. In exchange for survival into old age, men will have to relinquish some of their power and privilege. Such change means men must participate more fully in all dimensions of life with women and move beyond the rigid masculine roles that are doing them so much damage. They need to recognize and express emotions, function in multiple roles (including caregiving roles), connect with family and friends in more interdependent and intimate ways, and refuse to engage in risky habits and activities. Men must learn to control aggression and violence against themselves and others and to work for an end to violent aggression at all levels of society, from domestic violence to street violence to international war.

Quite often, women are advised to be more like men—to make themselves tougher, less emotional, more competitive, and less dependent on others, and to work longer hours. Yet the feminine qualities they would sacrifice in the process are the very things that seem to keep women alive. Feminine patterns of cooperation, health awareness, family attachment, friendship, nurturance, and multiple roles are the things that give women distinct health advantages. So in these ways, men would be well advised to be more like women rather than vice versa.

I realize that it is a tall order to convince men to give up the privilege and power that they've enjoyed in our patriarchal society. Yet these seductive advantages in early life are often the very experiences that render men vulnerable in the face of the discrimination they suffer in old age. The privilege and power men enjoy while young and able-bodied leave them ill prepared for the disempowerment and dependence they encounter in old age. Boys are taught and men believe the illusion that their worth as a person is in external control, domination, and power over others. Until they recognize that their real worth is internal, they'll be unprepared for the discrimination and invisibility they will face once they are old and without power. Such internal worth comes from finding diverse ways to adapt and relate to the environment and from building interdependent relationships with others.

I have watched older men struggle with age discrimination in public places like restaurants. As a woman, I've been ignored by service personnel all my life. When I enter a restaurant with an adult man, hostesses, waiters, and cashiers automatically assume that he's the person in charge of seat selection, ordering, paying, and tipping—that is, if he is under the age of seventy and is not noticeably disabled. When I eat out with an elderly person, man or woman, the same people who ignored me earlier now talk to me and assume that I'm in charge. They act like the older person isn't there or can't speak for him or herself. This is a form of impotence for older men that is rarely recognized or discussed. Though many men fear sexual impotence in their middle to late life, sexual impotence isn't as big of a threat to health and longevity as the more generalized impotence of age that older men encounter in a youth-oriented society. The loss of power and privilege after retirement is often very difficult for men and can leave them without hope or will to live. I believe that such feelings of impotence are at the heart of many of the suicides of older white males in this country.

Women are much better prepared to deal with age discrimination than are able-bodied, macho white men. Over a lifetime of suppression, women have learned coping skills and ways to survive in a sexist society that serve them well in an ageist society. By old age, many women feel more empowered than ever because they are freer than in their younger years, they know more about managing their lives, and they're well connected to family and friends. Men of the same age often feel like my poet and songwriter friend, Ric Masten:

THE DESERTED ROOSTER

if this were a documentary
Lorne Greene would narrate
describing in his big male animal world way
the migration
as one by one the fledglings flew the coop
followed by the hen
liberated and running off to join the sisters
cloistered in the halls
of a community college
singing
Gloria
Gloria
Steinem—till it becomes catholic

so far nothing new
children leaving home
a woman's victory
over the empty nest syndrome
themes done to death

but the deserted rooster is a subject
that has not yet been addressed
we know him
only as that laughable old strutter
preening and parading up and down
involved in his sexual prowess
and the sound of his own voice
up
at an ungodly hour to start the day

it was all part of the job
and there wasn't a problem
when there wasn't a choice

but picture him now
after the exodus

all alone
scratching around in his abandoned domain
looking for a good reason to get up tomorrow
and crow

if this were a documentary
it would end
focused on a stereotype weather vane
rusted on the turning point

in a changing wind

The world is changing rapidly. Women have been working hard to make some of those changes come about, especially in health and employment for women. Men are being left behind as they cling to old gender roles and expectations, to power and privilege. The damage this brings to men is showing up in the longevity statistics. Will men let the longevity gap continue to grow or will they wake up and look for answers to their own survival?

Some men resist change by digging in their heels and blaming women for their problems. Some pretend to change by drumming in the woods and playing warrior on the weekends, with either the mythopoetic men's movement begun by poet Robert Bly or with the militia groups that are preparing for battle with the government. Some gather in football fields to profess rigid religious beliefs and call for a return to former times where men ruled the household and the world. But until men really take daily action to stop killing themselves and join women as equal partners in all dimensions of life, they won't succeed in closing the longevity gap that started growing a half-century ago. The few men who have beaten the odds for survival and are living into very old age are the role models to study for guidance in finding new ways to be masculine.

CHARACTERISTICS OF
LONG-LIVED PEOPLE

In the past few years, I have been interviewing men and women over the age of eighty to understand their personal perspectives on growing old and to discover their secrets for living long and well. These long-lived people are good examples for younger generations and I've wanted to know what has enabled these particular people to survive into very old age. I ask them about their health and well-being in the physical, emotional, intellectual, social, occupational, spiritual, and environmental dimensions of their lives.

Among these elders, the men seem to be much like the women. Whether they always had more feminine patterns than other men or whether they have changed from their younger days is difficult to say, but at this late stage of life they have adopted many of the health-promoting characteristics that I have discussed in earlier chapters. As I've come to know these inspiring older people, I've detected at least four characteristics that most of them exhibit in all the dimensions of their lives. These qualities of living long and well have been touched on earlier in the book, but let's look at them again, in conclusion. They are flexibility, resiliency, connectedness, and enthusiastic engagement with life.

Flexibility

Almost everyone will tell you that to stay flexible is a good thing, but they are usually referring to physical flexibility. While toning and stretching exercises are very good for people of all ages, flexibility is equally or even more important in the other dimensions of life. Rigidity of body, mind, or spirit is deadly for people of any age—but is especially destructive to the health of elders.

As people age, they begin to lose many important things that they've taken for granted—things like their health, their friends and loved ones, and their roles in life. These losses can be overwhelming and may result in devastating grief and depression. For others, bitterness and anger are the pitfalls of such losses. When a person gets stuck in one emotional state, his or her well-being is at stake. Flexibility in emotional health requires that men and women grieve fully for their losses and feel appropriate anger for the injustices that age brings, but also work at finding joy, laughter, and humor in their aging life experiences. The ability to feel mad, glad, and sad and to avoid getting locked into one emotional state is necessary if one is to stay mentally fit. An optimistic outlook on life, in spite of adversity, has been found consistently among people who live into their nineties and beyond.

Flexibility in roles, learning, spiritual awareness, and relationships requires that men and women constantly assess their old patterns of doing things and consider new or different views and actions. For example, in some earlier research on loneliness in older adults, I discovered that those who were able to make new friends when they moved into a retirement center were much happier and significantly less lonely than those who struggled to maintain only their old relationships outside the center. Of course, new friends are not comparable to old, long-term relationships, but those who are flexible enough to cultivate both new and old friends throughout life are happier and build stronger support systems.

Rigid belief systems often break down when things go wrong in life. Flexibility in spiritual or religious beliefs enables the older person to accept the inevitable losses and tolerate the increased diversity encountered in new living environments or in an ever-changing world. For example, I recently learned of a ninety-six-year-old woman who set a model of tolerance and unconditional love for her whole family when her thirty-year-old granddaughter revealed that she was lesbian. All the other relatives in the family were shocked and troubled by this revelation, but this very aged grandmother was accepting and understanding of her granddaughter. From her perspective of ninety-six years, her granddaughter's sexual orientation was curious and unusual, but not something that was all that important to get upset about and certainly not something that would cause her to love her granddaughter any less.

Resilience

For many years, research on healthy people has emphasized the concept of *hardiness*. Hardiness implies the ability to resist disease and withstand stress, or in Darwinian terms, to be fit as in "survival of the fittest." The original research on hardiness was done on white male business executives. When these studies were replicated on women and other populations, the researchers did not get the same results. Women did not seem to be hardy in the same way that men were. This presented a dilemma. If men were hardier than women, why did they die earlier?

In recent years, the term *resilience* has begun to replace the term *hardiness,* and this seems to be the better concept to explain gender differences in longevity. To be resilient is to be able to recover from misfortune and to creatively live life in spite of disease and stress. Women seem to be more resilient and men more hardy.

The people I have interviewed who have lived long often do not report that they have been particularly hardy individuals, but they have all been resilient. Some may have been hardy like the mighty oak but most are like the toy Bozo the Clown, who always pops back up no matter how many times he gets knocked down. Many are living with chronic illnesses or have suffered serious health problems or major life traumas. Yet they manage to recover and to go on with life in positive, satisfying ways.

Another way to think of resilience is in terms of the ability to adapt to a system. Ecologist and psychotherapist Sarah A. Conn discusses the importance of survival in terms of "fitting in." Rather than the old competitive notion of survival of the fittest, the longevity of a species seems to be based more on ability to be open to and to contribute to the well-being of the whole system—to fit in constructively rather than to be independently hardy or dominant. This concept incorporates the qualities of flexibility and resilience that I see in many long-lived women and men.

Connectedness

Women and men who live long and well are not loners. They are connected to self, others, ideas, the earth, and the universe. They truly exemplify the self-in-relation model of identity that I describe in Chapter Two. They express few regrets in life and are secure in themselves. Though some may have been fiercely independent at earlier ages, they have survived the ravages of life by being dependent on others at times when they could not manage alone. Rather than resist this dependence, they have accepted it and felt grateful for the help they received from others. In old age, they readily recognize their connection with and need for others and have come to rely on the support systems that they have built throughout their lifetimes.

Most older people that I've met are opinionated but are also open to the ideas of others. They have an acceptance of their place in the world and of the inevitability of death. They grieve for the loved ones they've lost but continue to be interested in the friends and family who remain in their lives.

Engagement with Life

One of the earliest theories of aging assumed that elders would give up their roles in life and disengage from former activities. This theory of disengagement does not fit the elders I interviewed for my longevity project. These women and men were all engaged in life experiences at whatever level their health and economic resources would allow. Of course, all the elders who volunteered to be interviewed for my longevity project were certainly engaged with life or they wouldn't have been interested in participating in a research program. Most of the women and men I interviewed were living in their own homes or apartments in the community and were active in volunteer work, social events, and family affairs. However, even the people I see in retirement centers and nursing homes, if they aren't in severe pain or in the last stages of dementia, are also engaged with life within the context of their surroundings.

When I first began working with elders, I assumed that no one wanted to be in a nursing home. I found out that I was wrong. Many people who have lived in difficult surroundings welcome the care they get in a good nursing home. I've seen former bag ladies, lonely widowers, and women who have been afraid for their safety who are grateful and pleased to have a safe, clean, social environment in which to live out the remaining years of their lives. The nursing home is their home and the staff and other residents become their friends and family. From the outside, looking in, retirement centers and nursing homes may look like places where people go to die, but from the inside they are often lively places, filled with the drama of life. In well-managed, caring facilities, residents are able to stay engaged with life for much longer than they ever would be able to if they were left isolated and alone in the larger community.

Retirement centers often provide the support needed for the basic necessities of life like meals, housekeeping, and health care, so that elders can have time and energy left for the things that truly enhance life—socializing, recreation, educational programs, and cultural activities. In retirement centers, it is not at all uncommon to have residents who live to be a hundred years old or even older.

ROLE MODELS FOR LIVING LONG AND WELL

The following stories are of some of my interviewees, women and men who exhibit all four life-enhancing characteristics. Nancy is an example of a person who is living long and loving it. She is quite opinionated, yet she also is tolerant of others. She has friends of all ages and is certainly enthusiastic about her various activities.

Nancy has a sparkle in her eye and a spring in her step when she breezes into a room. She likes to shock others by her forthright statements. "At eighty-five, sex is not over! I am fortunate above most women that I am eighty-five and having such an interesting life sexually. I've never compared notes with my friends but I think I'm unusual. It's just plain bragging on my part." She goes on to describe several men that she has been friends with over the years since her husband died forty years ago. "Why would I want to remarry? Men and women should live next door to each other and visit."

Nancy stays busy with her many volunteer duties at several local agencies. She is a political activist, a feminist, and pro-choice. She states, "I don't do so much volunteer work now but I go down when Planned Parenthood is expecting some trouble because they know that I'm always ready to be arrested if necessary. . . . To some extent I find that I still have the tough-mindedness that I've always had.

"The priest is my next door neighbor and we're friends. He tells me that he always prays for sinners and that he's praying for me. We never really argue. He never queries me about my work in Planned Parenthood and I don't try to destroy his faith." She goes on to say, "Oh, to be seventy-five again. When I was sixty I was the most busy. I can't do that now. I have friends who play bridge three times a week. I can't imagine anything less productive."

In answering questions about her health, she says, "My diet is splendid. I love to cook. . . . I love high-class coffee and vegetables and fruits. I'm an aristocrat about food. . . . I average three or four cigarettes a month with my martinis. I'm a social drinker. I usually drink Scotch when I have dinner guests but only the best Scotch and I want a martini with the best gin. I don't prostitute myself with my liquor. I do ten minutes of exercise a day to limber up. When I had eye surgery I couldn't do my exercises and I felt like an old woman for the first time. I creaked."

About her own longevity, she says, "My friends are all dying off—doggone it. They'll miss me when I'm gone. I've got a lot of awards because of my longevity but I expect to die someday. It seems highly improbable but I guess it will happen. I don't plan to become infirm and in a nursing home. I have my plans all made. I let my friends know when I plan to be gone because one time they broke into my house when they hadn't heard from me because they thought that I may have fallen or something. I was so touched by that."

Nancy's only real regret is that she didn't get to go to medical school. "I'm a frustrated brain surgeon." She surrounds herself with educated, intelligent people. "I only tolerate the nincompoops. I try to be polite but I try not to spend much time with them." She cries when she is upset or infuriated but doesn't "sit around sniveling." "Pride has kept me going." She has a good but "peculiar" sense of humor, which has "turned bitter around the edges because of the fallibility of a whole bunch of humankind."

According to Nancy, women live longer than men because "men are such stubborn mules that they don't take care of themselves as we women do. . . . They don't even have doctors who know them."

Nancy exemplifies enthusiastic engagement with living. She pays attention to her physical health and is especially pleased that she continues to be able to express her sexuality. For many older women, this is not an option because there are so few available men or their personal values will not allow them to have sex outside marriage. Nancy's social health, her intellectual well-being, and her mental health are also her strong points. Her many volunteer activities give her a strong sense of worth and purpose. She indicates that life will not be worth living if she ever becomes ill and dependent. She hinted at taking her own life in that event, but she was not specific about how she would accomplish that.

Jed has lived as long as Nancy and savors life just as much, even though he has had very different experiences. He has had to be flexible throughout his long life. His resilience and optimistic attitude in spite of several serious health problems keep him involved with friends and many social activities.

Though eighty-five-year-old Jed has had to use a scooter to get around since a stroke in 1985 left him unable to walk, he still considers himself one of the luckiest guys who ever lived. "I'm lucky for two reasons: the family I was born into and the era that I have lived. During my lifetime there has been more advancement of the human race than in any comparable period in history."

His work history has been extremely varied. He received a degree in mechanical engineering during the Depression but was never able to find work in the field, so he worked in factories, sold insurance and real estate, and made deliveries on a bakery route, eventually establishing an ice cream and sandwich shop before he was drafted into the Army during World War II. He spent five years in the service as a drill sergeant at different bases in the States and then as a radar repairman in Okinawa. He says, "The draft seemed unfair to me. I was married and had a business and then was drafted with a pay of $21 a month. When I was in Okinawa, I read that people back here in the shipyards were striking for more pay. I had no chance for an increase. It soured me on unions because they were striking when we needed stuff to fight with."

After returning from the war, he owned a variety of businesses where his wife worked with him as an equal partner. His only regret in life is that when his wife got pregnant the first time, they decided to get an abortion. After that she could not have any more children. "I'm pro-choice but I still regret that decision." His wife died six years ago and he has lived alone since that time.

"I'm not a religious person. I would be classified as an agnostic. My grandmother was a Quaker. Mother attended a Christian church and my wife was a Lutheran, but I would only go to church occasionally.

"I have firm notions on politics. I'm conservative. For example, I think Franklin Roosevelt was the poorest president we ever had. . . . He was a complete dud. . . . On the abortion issue I have a liberal view, but that's the only one."

Jed stays in touch with old friends and is actively involved with many social activities. He showed us a picture of his old high school classmates, who meet for breakfast on the second Tuesday of every month. "Now, everyone in that picture would be eighty-five years or older," he says, rather surprised himself at how old everyone is. He plays euchre about five times a week with three different groups of people. He drives himself to all his social activities in a van especially equipped with a lift for his scooter.

The pain of being male is his earliest memory. "I remember being circumcised at two years of age. It hurt me. . . . It was the first and worst time I've ever been hurt in my life."

His health habits have improved over the years. "I eat any damn thing I want, which includes a lot of beef, quite a few berries, and pasta. I cook all my food. . . . I find it's much easier to cook a meal than to get to a restaurant. . . . I don't walk worth a damn." He remembers age forty-nine as being a particularly bad year for him because he got his first pair of glasses, had a heart attack, and had to get false teeth. "I damn near fell apart. But now, other than not being able to walk, I'm doing fine." He doesn't get much exercise but at age sixty, before his stroke, he was walking three miles a day. "I smoked about fifty years . . . rolled my own cigarettes, smoked a pipe and cigars. I never could see that it hurt me any." But he quit twenty years ago when he realized that he didn't have much control over his own addiction. "I couldn't seem to quit . . . so when I got mad about it I finally did quit. . . . I've never quit drinking though. I drink whiskey about every day. One or two drinks a day for most of my life. I kind of like it."

About his own longevity, he believes, "I've lived so long because of my easy-going nature, I guess. . . . I don't tend to get excited about things. I let things run off my back like water off a duck's back." He copes with his wife's death because "there's nothing you can do about it. Grown men don't cry, though I've been guilty of it, particularly at my wife's funeral." He thinks that a sense of humor helps him survive. "If you can't have a little fun in life there's no use living," he says. He ended the interview with the statement, "I've had a long life . . . a good life. I have no enemies that I know of."

Because of Jed's disability and various illnesses, he did not consider remarriage after his wife died. This is unusual for a man who survives his spouse, as most men prefer marriage to living alone. Jed's strengths are his emotional and social well-being. He takes things as they come and he stays connected to old friends, as well as keeping active with more recent acquaintances.

Lester is an example of a man who has lived a long life in relatively good health. As a farmer, laborer, horseman, and businessman, he led a very masculine lifestyle. However, since his wife died and he moved to a retirement center, he has been surrounded by women and has adapted to activities that might be described as more feminine. He continues to have many interests and hobbies, though he complains that he has had to slow down in recent years.

Ninety-seven-year-old Lester welcomes the chance to talk about his life at every opportunity. His apartment is homey but cluttered with his hobbies. The first thing he likes to show visitors is the latest quilt he is working on. His two passions in recent years are dancing and quilting. He keeps a small portable sewing machine in his bedroom, where he pieces together patchwork quilts of different sizes and designs, which he then gives to friends or donates to different causes. In between making his quilts, having lunch with friends, and going to church on Sundays, he dances every chance he gets. A new woman who also loves to dance has recently moved into the retirement center where he lives, so even though she is twenty years younger, they have formed a close relationship around this common interest. "This relationship is not serious but she's a good dancer. She's a good scout. She was a ballet dancer as a girl," he explains.

He attributes his long life to hard work, good health habits, and emotional stability. "I've lived a pretty clean life. I've lived outdoors. I don't smoke. I don't allow myself to get excited. I had a few scraps but I got out of fights by bluffing. I like to take a drink now and then but I never got drunk in my whole life. I always knew when to quit. I've worked real, real hard. Hard work don't hurt nobody," he adds as he describes his life on the farm and working on the railroad.

Like most of the elder men we interviewed, Lester had a variety of jobs throughout his life. In addition to farm work and hard labor, he also worked for a state highway department and trained and raced horses. The horse business is how he made money enough to enjoy a good old age and his love of horses kept him racing until age ninety-two. He held the track record for surrey racing for over a year. For the past five years, he has continued to hang out at the racetrack, but only assists the other jockeys with their horses. "I had a lot of horse sense and a lot of horse knowledge. I even rodeoed a little before I got married," he remembers.

Although he never had any children of his own, he and his wife raised three orphan children. "We never needed to have our own because we had kids to peddle," he says as he describes the children who liked to visit his horse ranch. These kids are now senior citizens themselves but they continue to visit him, so that he never lacks company. His adopted son wants him to come and live with him in another state, but Lester wants to stay independent, so he compromises and goes to visit him several times a year.

When asked about the most influential person or experience in his life, he talked about his friendship with the Cisco Kid, a popular entertainment figure, who spent two summers on Lester's horse farm. He denounces the other men in the retirement center because they don't stay active. "They sit down and hope to die. I'm having a good time and I'm going to have a good time as long as I'm breathing."

Lester is similar to Nancy in that his many productive activities and his social life keep him feeling energized and connected. He, too, has never remarried after his wife's death, but, unlike Jed, has chosen not to live alone but to move into a retirement village where all the basic necessities like shopping, cooking, and cleaning are taken care of by others, so that he is free to enjoy a wide variety of meaningful activities. Ninety-three-year-old Elsie is an example of someone who continues to live as fully as she can even though she has suffered physical illness and mental confusion at times (as a result of a stroke) and has recently been moved into a nursing home.

> "Mother always called me the light-hearted one. I was the happy-go-lucky one," says ninety-three-year-old Elsie as she describes her growing up in a family of four children. Today she uses a walker to get around the nursing home where she has lived for a year, since suffering a blackout in her home, where she had lived alone for twenty-three years after her husband died.
>
> "I am big enough to give it up," she says in describing the decision to leave her house. Now she enjoys the attention she gets from the staff. "The aides love to come to my room when they have free time because I'm a lot of fun to talk with," she brags. Her son visits her every day and she talks with her daughter several times a week. She has made a few friends in the nursing home and looks forward to regular visits from her grandchildren.
>
> Her greatest love is singing. She remembers that her mother used to punish her for singing too much as a child. As an adult she has sung in choirs and quartets. She describes herself as a "calm, easy-going person" who loves to laugh. "I cry sometimes too, though, when I think about the good times I had with my family in our home."
>
> She says that women live longer than men because "women really run things. I had a good, happy marriage that lasted a long time because I was in charge and was the boss. That was good for everybody's health."

Elsie's strengths are her resilience in spite of her recent problems and her strong connections to her family and staff at the nursing home. She loves people more than she loves material possessions, so though it was difficult to leave her home, she adjusted and looked for ways to make her new living environment a positive, meaningful place for her life. Unlike Nancy, she feels that a nursing home is a good place to be and would never consider ending her life because of illness and dependence.

These four examples are a very small sample of the many, many elders who still love life and live it to the fullest. When young people look through the lens of an ageist society, any one of these people might be considered old, ugly, or useless, but to talk to them and learn about their lives, ideas, hopes, and dreams is to realize that aging, while it has its problems, also has many joys and satisfactions. By such very old ages, the gender differences have faded and these men and women are living in the moment for as long as they have left. They have little time or patience for regrets, prejudices, or facades.

CHOICES

At this point in history, it seems that our society has come to a fork in the gender road and the way we go will determine if the gender gap in longevity will widen or close. One path will lead to even greater gender conflicts. If men do not change from their old role behaviors, there will be greater divisions between men and women in all dimensions of life. Women will continue to expand their roles and options and will lose hope that men will ever participate as equal partners in life.

The other path will lead us to greater cooperation, equality, and understanding between men and women. If men make the necessary changes, if they reject the old-style masculinity that damages their health, then I have great hope that future generations of men and women will find ways to come together as we have never been able to in history. With positive, nondestructive masculine and feminine energies working to improve life, we'll all be able to live long and love it as we learn to love ourselves and each other.

At times, I despair that men aren't ready to make these changes, but there are glimmerings of movement toward such goals. The National Organization for Men Against Sexism (NOMAS) was organized in 1982. Their informational brochure states: "The traditional male role has steered many men into patterns such as isolation from children, lack of close relationships, denying of feelings, competitiveness, aggressiveness, preoccupation with work and success. NOMAS believes that men can live happier and more fulfilled lives by challenging, and unlearning, many of the old lessons of traditional masculinity."

The American Psychological Association has recently established a new division called the Society for the Psychological Study of Men and Masculinity, and I'm hopeful that other proactive groups are organizing as well. But it will take a major groundswell of action soon to make the kind of strides that our society needs.

One thing is for sure. We cannot and will not return to the sexism and the sex roles of the past. The women's movement has changed our lives and our times. Women's lives and longevity are better than ever before. It is time for men to decide if they want to change and save

themselves. Another poem by Ric Masten captures the dilemma that
many men face today.

A VANISHING SPECIES

I was born on a planet
over fifty light-years from here

an idyllic world
where children grew up
without the threat of nuclear holocaust
or ecological strangulation
no instant systems of communication
no black revolutions
gay revolutions
no women's liberation
not even the choice
of taking or not taking the pill
an Eden really

true
the seed of all this was there
but had nothing to do
with my first fifteen years

and now
I find myself come to this harsh place
a kind of space traveler
having close encounters with my own children
like creatures
from different star systems
we stare at each other
across the void
even our words have different
stems

we are aliens in each other's midst

but damn it
I am the one saddled with the memory
of that other place

part of a colony
stranded on the planet earth
toward the end of the twentieth century
marooned
with no way to go back
and no time to go on

like a moon being eclipsed
my kind will soon be gone
and in light
of the headlines today
the sooner the better

I began by saying that my goals for writing this book were to validate women's experiences and to alert men to the damage they're doing to their own health and survival by clinging to an outdated style of masculinity. For the sake of our society, our environment, and the survival of my son, my grandsons, and all good men, I hope that I have been successful. My love of women and men alike and my hope for our future cause me to sound this alarm and offer these challenges for men to learn from women some ways in which to live longer. If men are successful in making such changes, life will be better for us all.

~~~ References

Chapter One

Friedan, B. (1983). *The feminine mystique.* New York: Dell. (Reprinted with permission.)

McGrath, E., Keita, G. P., Strickland, B. R., & Russo, N. F. (1990). *Women and depression: Risk factors and treatment issues.* Washington, DC: American Psychological Association.

Montague, A. (1974). *The natural superiority of women.* New York: Macmillan.

U.S. Bureau of the Census. (1992). *1990 census of population: General population characteristics.* Washington, DC: U.S. Government Printing Office.

U.S. Bureau of the Census. (1994). *Statistical abstract of the United States: 1994* (Vol. 114). Washington, DC: U.S. Government Printing Office.

Chapter Two

Andres, R. (1994). Mortality and obesity: The rationale for age-specific height-weight tables. In W. R. Hazzard, E. L. Bierman, J. P. Blass, W. H. Ettinger Jr., & J. B. Halter (Eds.), *Geriatric medicine and gerontology* (3rd ed.). New York: McGraw-Hill.

Dabbs, J. M., & Morris, R. (1990). Testosterone, social class, and antisocial behavior in a sample of 4,462 men. *Psychological Science, 1*(3), 209–211.

Doress-Worters, P. B., & Siegal, D. L. (1994). *The new ourselves, growing older.* New York: Simon & Schuster.

Gutmann, D. L. (1987). *Reclaimed powers: Toward a new psychology of men and women in late life.* New York: Basic Books.

Hazzard, W. R. (1994). The sex differences in longevity. In W. R. Hazzard, E. L. Bierman, J. P. Blass, W. H. Ettinger Jr., & J. B. Halter (Eds.), *Geriatric medicine and gerontology* (3rd ed.). New York: McGraw-Hill.

Martin, G. M., & Turker, M. S. (1994). Genetics of human disease, longevity, and aging. In W. R. Hazzard, E. L. Bierman, J. P. Blass, W. H. Ettinger Jr., & J. B. Halter (Eds.), *Geriatric medicine and gerontology* (3rd ed.). New York: McGraw-Hill.

Miller, J. B. (1976). *Toward a new psychology of women.* Boston: Beacon Press.

Neel, J. V. (1990). Toward an explanation of the human sex ratio. In M. G. Ory & H. R. Warner (Eds.), *Gender, health, and longevity.* New York: Springer.

Neugarten, B. L., & Gutmann, D. L. (1964). Age-sex roles and personality in middle age: A thematic apperception study. In B. L. Neugarten & Associates (Eds.), *Personality in middle and late life.* New York: Atherton.

Paganini-Hill, A., & Henderson, V. W. (1994). Estrogen deficiency and risk of Alzheimer's disease. *American Journal of Epidemiology, 140,* 254–261.

Sheehy, G. (1995). *New passages: Mapping your life across time.* New York: Random House.

Shimokata, H., Tobin, J. D., Muller, D. C., Elahi, D., Coon, P. J., & Andres, R. (1989). Studies in the distribution of body fat: I. Effects of age, sex, and obesity. *Journal of Gerontology: Medical Sciences, 44,* M66–M73.

Travis, C. B. (1988). *Women and health psychology: Biomedical issues.* Hillsdale, NJ: Erlbaum.

Weksler, M. E. (1990). A possible role for the immune system in the gender-longevity differential. In M. G. Ory & H. R. Warner (Eds.), *Gender, health, and longevity.* New York: Springer.

Chapter Three

Crose, R., Duffy, M., Warren, J., & Franklin, B. (1987). Project OASIS: Volunteer mental health paraprofessionals serving nursing home residents. *Gerontologist, 27,* 359–362.

Crose, R., Nicholas, C., Gobble, D., & Frank, B. (1992). Gender and wellness: A multidimensional systems model for counseling. *Journal of Counseling and Development, 71,* 149–156.

Nicholas, D., Gobble, D., Crose, R., & Frank, B. (1992). A systems view of health, wellness, and gender: Implications for mental health counseling. *Journal of Mental Health Counseling, 14,* 8–19.

Chapter Four

Ayanian, J. Z., & Epstein, A. M. (1991). Differences in the use of procedures between women and men hospitalized for coronary heart disease. *New England Journal of Medicine, 325,* 221–225.

Drewnowski, A., & Yee, D. K. (1987). Men and body image: Are males satisfied with their body weight? *Psychosomatic Medicine, 49,* 626–634.

Flaming, D., & Morse, J. M. (1991). Minimizing embarrassment: Boys' experiences of pubertal changes. *Issues in Comprehensive Pediatric Nursing, 14,* 211–230.

Goldberg, K. (1993). *How men can live as long as women: Seven steps to a longer and better life.* Fort Worth, TX: Summit Group.

Gutmann, D. L. (1987). *Reclaimed powers: Toward a new psychology of men and women in late life.* New York: Basic Books.

Leigh, J. P., & Fries, J. F. (1992–1993). Associations among healthy habits, age, gender, and education in a sample of retirees. *International Journal of Aging and Human Development, 36,* 139–155.

McAuley, W. J., Travis, S. S., & Safewright, M. (1990). The relationship between formal and informal health care services for the elderly. In S. M. Stahl (Ed.), *The legacy of longevity: Health and health care in later life.* Thousand Oaks, CA: Sage.

Robinson, J. P., & Godbey, G. (1993). Sport, fitness, and the gender gap. *Leisure Sciences, 15,* 291–307.

Rolls, B. J., Fedoroff, I. C., & Guthrie, J. F. (1991). Gender differences in eating behavior and body weight regulation. *Health Psychology, 10,* 133–142.

Shephard, R. J., & Montelpare, W. (1988). Geriatric benefits of exercise as an adult. *Journal of Gerontology: Medical Sciences, 43,* M86–M90.

Silberstein, L. R., Striegel-Moore, R. H., Timko, C., & Rodin, J. (1988). Behavioral and psychological implications of body dissatisfaction: Do men and women differ? *Sex Roles, 19,* 219–232.

Smith, D.W.E. *(1993). Human longevity.* New York: Oxford University Press.

Stein, J. H., & Reiser, L. W. (1994). A study of white middle-class adolescent boys' responses to "semenarche" (the first ejaculation). *Journal of Youth and Adolescence, 23,* 373–384.

Travis, C. B. (1988). *Women and health psychology: Biomedical issues.* Hillsdale, NJ: Erlbaum.

U.S. Department of Health and Human Services. (1994). *Epidemiologic trends in drug abuse. Vol. 1: Highlights and executive summary* (NIH

Publication No. 95–3988). Washington, DC: U.S. Government Printing Office.

U.S. Department of Health and Human Services. (1994). *National household survey on drug abuse: Population estimates 1993* (DHHS Publication No. SMA 94–3017). Washington, DC: U.S. Government Printing Office.

Waldron, I. (1976). Why do women live longer than men? *Social Science & Medicine, 10,* 349–362.

Waldron, I. (1983). Sex differences in illness incidence, prognosis and mortality: Issues and evidence. *Social Science & Medicine, 17,* 1107–1123.

Wenger, N. K., Speroff, L., & Packard, B. (1993). Cardiovascular health and disease in women. *New England Journal of Medicine, 329,* 247–256.

Yalom, M., Estler, S., & Brewster, W. (1982). Changes in female sexuality: A study of mother/daughter communication and generational differences. *Psychology of Women Quarterly, 7,* 141–154.

Chapter Five

Hayes, E., & Baldwin, J. (1993). The gender gap: Women and men who take the GED tests. In *GED profiles: Adults in transition, 6.* Washington, DC: American Council on Education.

Johnson, E. H. (1990). *The deadly emotions: The role of anger, hostility, and aggression in health and emotional well-being.* New York: Praeger.

Kroll, B., & Baldwin, J. (1994). GED candidates: Does age make a difference? In *GED profiles: Adults in transition, 7.* Washington, DC: American Council on Education.

Longino, C. F., Jr. (1990). The relative contributions of gender, social class, and advancing age to health. In S. M. Stahl (Ed.), *The legacy of longevity: Health and health care in later life.* Thousand Oaks, CA: Sage.

McGrath, E., Keita, G. P., Strickland, B. R., & Russo, N. F. (1990). *Women and depression: Risk factors and treatment issues.* Washington, DC: American Psychological Association.

McIntosh, J. L., Santos, J. F., Hubbard, R. W., & Overholser, J. C. (1994). *Elder suicide: Research, theory, and treatment.* Washington, DC: American Psychological Association.

Temoshok, L., & Dreher, H. (1992). *The Type C connection: The behavioral links to cancer and your health.* New York: Random House.

Temoshok, L., Van Dyke, C., & Zegans, L. S. (Eds.). (1983). *Emotions in health and illness: Theoretical and research foundations.* Philadelphia: Grune & Stratton.

Travis, C. B. (1988). *Women and health psychology: Mental health issues.* Hillsdale, NJ: Erlbaum.

Chapter Six

Connidis, I. A., & Davies, L. (1990). Confidants and companions in later life: The place of family and friends. *Journal of Gerontology: Social Sciences, 45,* S141–S149.

Kendig, H. L., Coles, R., Pittelkow, Y., & Wilson, S. (1988). Confidants and family structure in old age. *Journal of Gerontology: Social Sciences, 43,* S31–S40.

Lips, H. M. (1991). *Women, men, and power.* Mountain View, CA: Mayfield.

Montgomery, R., & Datwyler, M. M. (1990). Women and men in the caregiving role. *Generations, 14*(3), 34–38.

Chapter Seven

American Association for Retired Persons. (1995). *A profile of older Americans.* Washington, DC: Author.

Faludi, S. (1991). *Backlash: The undeclared war against American women.* New York: Crown.

Chapter Eight

Erikson, E. (1963). *Childhood and society.* New York: Norton.

Kivett, V. R. (1979). Religious motivation in middle age: Correlates and implications. *Journal of Gerontology, 34,* 106–115.

Levin, J. S., Taylor, R. J., & Chatters, L. M. (1994). Race and gender differences in religiosity among older adults: Findings from four national surveys. *Journal of Gerontology: Social Sciences, 49,* S137–S145.

McStay, J. R., & Dunlap, R. E. (1983). Male-female differences in concern for environmental quality. *International Journal of Women's Studies, 6,* 291–301.

Neugarten, B. L., & Associates (Eds.). (1964). *Personality in middle and late life.* New York: Atherton.

Pollan, S. M., & Levine, M. (1995). Die broke. *Worth, 4*(6), 56–66.

Rodin, J., & Langer, E. (1977). Long-term effects of a control-relevant intervention with the institutionalized aged. *Journal of Personality and Social Psychology, 35,* 897–902.

Wilson, J., & Sherkat, D. E. (1994). Returning to the fold. *Journal for the Scientific Study of Religion, 33,* 148–161.

Chapter Nine

Bureau of Justice Statistics. (1994). *Sourcebook of criminal justice statistics.* Washington, DC: U.S. Department of Justice.

Centers for Disease Control. (1989). *The national nursing home survey: 1985 summary for the United States* (DHHS Publication No. PHS 89–1758). Washington, DC: U.S. Department of Health and Human Services.

Conn, S. A. (1995). When the earth hurts, who responds? In T. Roszak, M. E. Gomes, & A. D. Kanner (Eds.), *Ecopsychology: Restoring the earth, healing the mind.* San Francisco: Sierra Club.

Cumming, E., & Henry, W. (1961). *Growing old.* New York: Basic Books.

Kobasa, S. C. (1979). Stressful life events, personality, and health: An inquiry into hardiness. *Journal of Personality and Social Psychology, 37,* 1–11.

Masten, R. (1990). "The deserted rooster." *Ric Masten speaking.* Watsonville, CA: Papier-Mâché Press.

Masten, R. (1990). "A vanishing species." *Ric Masten speaking.* Watsonville, CA: Papier-Mâché Press.

National Organization for Men Against Sexism. (n.d.). *National Organization for Men Against Sexism: NOMAS.* [Brochure]. Ashtabula, OH: Author.

~~~ Further Resources

Barnett, R. C., Biener, L., & Baruch, G. K. (Eds.). (1987). *Gender and stress: The groundbreaking investigation of how stress is caused and experienced—differently—in the lives of women and men.* New York: Free Press.

Belenky, M. F., Clinchy, B. M., Goldberger, N. R., & Tarule, J. M. (1986). *Women's ways of knowing: The development of self, voice, and mind.* New York: Basic Books.

Bem, S. L. (1993). *The lenses of gender: Transforming the debate on sexual inequality.* New Haven, CT: Yale University Press.

Bronte, L. (1993). *The longevity factor: The new reality of long careers and how it can lead to richer lives.* New York: Harper Perennial.

Brooks, G. R. (1995). *The centerfold syndrome: How men can overcome objectification and achieve intimacy with women.* San Francisco: Jossey-Bass.

Busse, E. W., & Maddox, G. L. (1985). *The Duke longitudinal studies of normal aging, 1955–1980.* New York: Springer.

Crose, R. (Ed.). (1993). *Gender and gerontology: Women's issues in mental health and lifespan development.* Muncie, IN: Institute of Gerontology, Ball State University.

Downes, P., Tuttle, I., Faul, P., & Mudd, V. (1996). *The new older woman: A dialogue for the coming century.* Berkeley, CA: Celestial Arts.

Dychtwald, K., & Flower, J. (1989). *Age wave: The challenges and opportunities of an aging America.* Los Angeles: Tarcher.

Evans, W., & Rosenberg, I. H. (1991). *Biomarkers: The ten keys to prolonging vitality.* New York: Simon & Schuster.

Fausto-Sterling, A. (1992). *Myths of gender: Biological theories about women and men.* New York: Basic Books.

Friedan, B. (1993). *The fountain of age.* New York: Simon & Schuster.

Gallagher, W. (1993). *The power of place: How our surroundings shape our thoughts, emotions, and actions.* New York: Poseidon Press.

Garner, J. D., & Mercer, S. O. (Eds.). (1989). *Women as they age: Challenge, opportunity and triumph.* New York: Haworth Press.

Garner, J. D., & Young, A. A. (Eds.). (1993). *Women and healthy aging: Living productively in spite of it all.* New York: Harrington Park Press.

Gilligan, C. (1982). *In a different voice: Psychological theory and women's development.* Cambridge, MA: Harvard University Press.

Grau, L. (Ed.). (1988). *Women in the later years: Health, social, and cultural perspectives.* New York: Harrington Park Press.

Hagan, K. L. (Ed.). (1992). *Women respond to the men's movement.* San Francisco: Harper San Francisco.

Hayflick, L. (1996). *How and why we age.* New York: Ballantine.

Hazzard, W. R., Bierman, E. L., Blass, J. P., Ettinger, W. H., Jr., & Halter, J. B. (Eds.). *Geriatric medicine and gerontology* (3rd ed.). New York: McGraw-Hill.

Herzog, A. R., Holden, K. C., & Seltzer, M. M. (Eds.). (1989). *Health and economic status of older women: Research issues and data sources.* Amityville, NY: Baywood.

Higgins, G. O. (1994). *Resilient adults: Overcoming a cruel past.* San Francisco: Jossey-Bass.

Hood, J. C. (Ed.). (1993). *Men, work, and family.* Thousand Oaks, CA: Sage.

Inlander, C. B., & Hodge, M. (1992). *100 ways to live to 100.* New York: Wings Books.

Jordan, J., Kaplan, A., Miller, J. B., Stiver, I. P., & Surrey, J. L. (Eds.). (1991). *Women's growth in connections: Writings from the Stone Center.* New York: Guilford Press.

Kaschak, E. (1992). *Engendered lives: A new psychology of women's experience.* New York: Basic Books.

Kohn, A. (1992). *No contest: The case against competition* (Rev. ed.). Boston: Houghton Mifflin.

Kottler, J.A. (1996). *The language of tears.* San Francisco: Jossey-Bass.

Levant, R. F., & Pollack, W. S. (Eds.). (1995). *A new psychology of men.* New York: Basic Books.

Ludwig, F. C. (Ed.). (1991). *Life span extension: Consequences and open questions.* New York: Springer.

Maccoby, E. E., & Jacklin, C. N. (1974). *The psychology of sex differences.* Stanford, CA: Stanford University Press.

McGrath, E. (1994). *When feeling bad is good: An innovative self-help program for women to convert "healthy" depression into new sources of growth and power.* New York: Bantam Books.

McLean, C., Carey, M., & White, C. (Eds.). (1996). *Men's ways of being.* Boulder, CO: Westview Press.

Miedzian, M. (1991). *Boys will be boys: Breaking the link between masculinity and violence.* New York: Doubleday.

Moore, T. J. (1993). *Lifespan: Who lives longer and why.* New York: Simon & Schuster.

Nardi, P. M. (Ed.). (1992). *Men's friendships.* Thousand Oaks, CA: Sage.

National Organization for Men Against Sexism (NOMAS), 2914 Northridge East, #315, Ashtabula, OH 44004.

Ory, M. G., & Warner, H. R. (Eds.). (1990). *Gender, health, and longevity: Multidisciplinary perspectives.* New York: Springer.

Peterson, W. A., & Quadagno, J. (Eds.). (1985). *Social bonds in later life: Aging and interdependence.* Thousand Oaks, CA: Sage.

Roberto, K. A. (Ed.). (1994). *Older women with chronic pain.* New York: Harrington Park Press.

Rosenthal, E. R. (Ed.). (1990). *Women, aging, and ageism.* New York: Harrington Park Press.

Ryan, R. S., & Travis, J. W. (1991). *Wellness: Small changes you can use to make a big difference.* Berkeley, CA: Ten Speed Press.

Society for the Psychological Study of Men and Masculinity (SPSMM), Division 51 of the American Psychological Association, 750 First Street NE, Washington, DC 20002.

Stahl, S. M. (Ed.). (1990). *The legacy of longevity: Health and health care in later life.* Thousand Oaks, CA: Sage.

Stevenson, M. R. (Ed.). (1994). *Gender roles through the life span: A multidisciplinary perspective.* Muncie, IN: Ball State University.

Tannen, D. (1994). *Talking from 9 to 5: Women and men in the workplace: Language, sex, and power.* New York: Avon Books.

Thompson, E. H., Jr. (1994). *Older men's lives.* Thousand Oaks, CA: Sage.

Turner, B. F., & Troll, L. E. (Eds.). (1994). *Women growing older: Psychological perspectives.* Thousand Oaks, CA: Sage.

Unger, R. K. (Ed.). (1989). *Representations: Social constructions of gender.* Amityville, NY: Baywood.

Van Dyke, C., Temoshok, L., & Zegans, L. S. (Eds.). (1984). *Emotions in health and illness: Applications to clinical practice.* Philadelphia: Grune & Stratton.

Walsh, M. R. (Ed.). (1987). *The psychology of women: Ongoing debates.* New Haven, CT: Yale University Press.

Walters, M., Carter, B., Papp, P., & Silverstein, O. (1988). *The invisible web: Gender patterns in family relationships.* New York: Guilford Press.

Wilbur, K. (1996). *A brief history of everything.* Boston: Shambhala.

Williams, C. L. (Ed.). (1993). *Doing "women's" work: Men in nontraditional occupations.* Thousand Oaks, CA: Sage.

Zanardi, C. (Ed.). (1990). *Essential papers on the psychology of women.* New York: New York University Press.

ᐧᐧᐧᐧ About the Author

Royda Crose, Ph.D., directs the Center for Gerontology and is associate director of the Fisher Institute for Wellness and associate professor of counseling psychology at Ball State University, Muncie, Indiana. She is a licensed psychologist and offers workshops, seminars, and lectures on the wellness model featured in this book through her consulting practice, "Heart-Land-Wisdom." She has published numerous manuscripts and book chapters on different aspects of psychology and aging and serves in many capacities for national and state organizations concerned with gerontology and psychology. Crose is a past coordinator for Psychologists in Long Term Care and is vice-chair of the Indiana Governor's Task Force for Alzheimer's Disease and Related Disorders. She is an appointed member of the Committee on Women in Psychology of the American Psychological Association.

Crose received her bachelor's degree in elementary education from the University of Tulsa, her master's degree in health education from Texas Woman's University, and her doctorate in counseling psychology from Texas A & M University. Before she entered graduate studies she held administrative positions in social service and health organizations in Dallas and New York City. In 1993, Crose participated in an educational exchange trip, lecturing in Japan and China on "Challenging Issues on Aging in the Coming Decades in the United States."

On a personal note, she is the proud mother of three grown children (a son, a daughter, and a daughter-in-law) and has four grandchildren. In planning for her own long life, she eventually hopes to retire to job opportunities that will allow her to continue writing, to travel the world, and to have many new and exciting adventures as she becomes an older, wiser, and more interesting woman.

━ᴡ━ Index

A

Accidents, automobile and work-related, 73
Ageism, 7, 142
Aggression: health effects of, 76; hormonal influences on, 29–30
Aging, positive aspects of, 7–9
Alcohol and drug use, 72–73
American Association for Retired People (AARP), 5
Andres, Reubin, 31
Anger, health effects of, 76
Autoimmune diseases, 26, 66

B

Baby boom generation: and changing roles of women, 13–14, 17–18; and menopause, 63–65
Baltimore Longitudinal Study on Aging, 31
Biology, and longevity, 2–3, 24–31

C

Caregiving: gender differences in, 106–107; by men, 52–53, 106–107; as occupation, 120–122; stress of, 109–110; by women, 16–17, 103–104
Centenarians, increase in, 1, 4–5
Chromosomes, and female advantage, 25, 28
Cigarette smoking, 71–72
Codependency, 33, 94–95
Conn, Sarah A., 147
Connectedness, 147

Cooperation, feminine model for, 97–98

D

Dabbs, James, 29
Deadly Emotions, The, 76
Death: elders' acceptance of, 138; leading causes of, 27; rates, and weight distribution, 31; of spouse, 82–83, 102–104, 152
Dependence/independence, 32, 33, 94–95, 147; in health management, 44
Depression: male, 80–81; peak periods of, 117; in women, 20, 64–65, 80–81
Diet, 67–69
Diseases: autoimmune, 26, 66; and body shape, 31; chronic, 66–67; and repression of emotion, 78; sex-linked, 25–26
Drug use, 72–73

E

Education, gender differences in, 87–88
Elder women, history and life experiences of, 9–14
Emotional well being: and emotional disorders, 80–87; and emotional expression, gender differences in, 76–79; and stress, 79–80. *See also* Mental health
Environmental well being, 48, 126–127; and living arrangements, 131–132, 133–135; and nurturing activities, 132–133; and sensory stimulation and deprivation, 133

Erikson, Erik, 127
Estrogen: buffering effects of, 27; replacement therapy, 28, 30
Exercise, 69–71

F

Faludi, Susan, 112–113
Family tradition, as legacy, 135–136
Feminine Mystique, The, 13
Financial resources: gender differences in, 122–124; as legacy, 135; management of, 122–124; overemphasis on, 110
Fisher Institute for Wellness, 44
Flexibility, 145–146
Food consumption: and nutrition, 67–69; sex differences in, 67–68
Friedan, Betty, 13
Friendship, gender differences in, 104–106

G

Gender, defined, 23
Gender characteristics, development of, 23–24
Gobble, David, 44

H

Hardiness, research on, 146
Hazzard, William R., 27
Health care, improvement in, 9–10
Health and wellness: dynamic, self-regulating properties of, 48–50; effects of life changes on, 19–20; habits, gender differences in, 65–74; individual approaches to, 36–44, 55
Hemophilia, 25
Holistic health, principles of, 44–50
Homemaking skills, 121
Homicidal behavior, 83–84
Hormone treatment: aversive, 29, 30; estrogen replacement, 28, 30
Hormones: buffering effects of estrogen, 27; and stress responses, 28–29; testosterone effects, 28–30
Hypochondriacs, 40–42, 66

I

Identity: and age discrimination, 142; development patterns, 32–34; in retirement, 19–20, 111, 118–119; self-in-relation model of, 34, 147; work-related, 112–114
Immunology, sex differences in, 26
Intellectual health, 47, 76, 87–93; and late-life learning, 90–93; teaching and mentoring activities, 91–93, 119–120
Interiority, 127
Intimacy, men's fear of, 84–85

J

Johnson, Ernest, 76

L

Learning, late-life, 90–93
Legacies, 127–128, 135–138
Life expectancy, average, 3–5
Lifestyles, gender differences in, 5–7
Living arrangements, 5–7, 131–132, 133–134
Longevity: behavioral, environmental, and personality factors in, 3, 31–34; biological influences on, 2–3, 24–31; connectedness as factor in, 147; and destructive habits, 71–73; and engagement with life, 147–148; gender gap in, 1–2, 4, 20, 25–31; and individual health-promoting characteristics, 144–148; and nature versus nurture debate, 2–3; role of resilience in, 146–147; and spiritual connections, 127, 129–131
Love, expression of, 84–87
Lung cancer, 72

M

Marriage: gender-based differences in, 99–101; remarriage patterns, 5–7, 152; and separation and divorce, 101–102; and widowhood, 5–6, 102–103
Masculinity: and competition, 95–97;

and dependence, 95; macho models of, 19, 84–85, 141, 142

Masten, Ric, 143–144, 156–157

Menopause, 63–65

Men's roles: as caregivers, 52–53, 106–107; change agenda in, 155–156; life-threatening aspects of, 18–20, 71–73; work-related, 19–20, 114–116

Menstruation, 56–59

Mental health, 75–93: and anger and aggression, 76; and connectedness and engagement with life, 147–148; and emotional disorders, 80–85; and individual's flexiblity, 145–146; and repressed hostility, 83; and resilience, 146–147; and sex differences in emotional expression, 46–47, 75–79, 84–87; sex differences in management of, 75; and stress, 47, 51, 79–80, 109; and suicidal behavior, 81–83

Midlife crisis, 63–65

Midlife women, history and life experiences of, 15–17

Miller, Jean Baker, 34

Money management, 122–124

Montague, Ashley, 13, 25

Morris, Robin, 29

N

National Organization for Men Against Sexism (NOMAS), 155

Natural Superiority of Women, The, 25

Nicholas, Donald, 44

Nursing homes, 18; environmental aspects of, 134–135; increase in, 140; positive aspects of, 148

Nurturing behaviors, as legacies, 136–138

P

Physical activity, gender differences in, 69–70

Physical appearance, developmental responses to, 60–61

Physical health, 46, 55–74; and exercise, 69–70; and help-seeking behaviors, 65–67; midlife concerns, 63–65; and nutrition, 67–68; of very old, 74

Pregnancy, male and female responses to, 61–63

Puberty, gender differences in, 56–60

R

Relationships, 46, 94–110; with adult children, 108–109; competition and cooperation in, 95–97; dependence/independence in, 32, 33, 44, 94–95, 147; empathy and problem-solving skills in, 98; of friendship, gender differences in, 104–106. *See also* Marriage

Religion, gender differences in, 47–48, 126, 127–131

Remarriage patterns, 5–7, 152

Reproductive health, 56–65; adolescent, 56–60; and physical development, 60–61; and pregnancy, 61–63; sex differential in, 56–65; stereotypes in, 56

Resilience, as longevity factor, 146–147

Retirement: and men's self-identity, 19–20; and power dynamics at home, 114–116

Retirement centers, positive experiences in, 148, 152–153

Risk-taking behaviors: and accidents, 73; hormonal influences on, 29–30; sex differential in, 71–74; substance abuse as, 72–73

Role models, 148–155

S

Schmottlach, Neil, 44

Sensory stimulation and deprivation, 133

Sex, defined, 23

Sex role differentiation, 32–33

Sexuality: elder, 149, 150; gender differences in, 84; and intimacy, 99; adolescent, 56–61

Spiritual well-being, 47–48, 126, 127–131

Stress: of caregiving, 109; effects of hormones on, 28–29; responses, sex differences in, 79–80; workplace, 47, 50

Suicidal behavior, 81–82

Support system, 50, 95; caregiving, 107; gender differences in, 107–108

T

Teaching and mentoring activities, 91–93, 119–120

Temoshok, Lydia, 78

Testosterone, effects of, 28–30

Tobin, Sheldon, 119

Travis, Cheryl Brown, 28–29

U

Undeclared War Against American Women, The, 112–113

V

Vietnam War, legacy of, 85

Violence, male, 73–74, 83

Volunteer counselors, 51–53

Volunteer work, 14

W

War, 73–74, 83–84

Weight: distribution, and illness, 31; gender differences in desired body image, 67

Wellness, life-span model of, 44–53

Widowhood, 102–104; gender gap in, 5–6

Women's movement, 13, 14, 57

Women's roles: continuity of, 119–120; dramatic changes in, 9, 12, 13; as family caregivers, 15, 16; multiple nature of, 111–112, 116–117; traditional, 114–116

Work roles: of elders, 120–122; gender differences in, 111–114; as identity, 109–110; male, 19–20, 115–116; traditional, 114–116; women's, 9, 12, 13, 111–112, 116–117, 119–120; and workplace economics, 112, 122–124; and workplace stress, 47, 50